To Joyce and Dan —

Proving that _old_

friends are at _ease_

with conversation!!

Bob Dwyer

CONVERSATIONS
with BOBBY
From Foster Child to Corporate Executive

Bob Danzig

CWLA
PRESS

ARLINGTON, VA

CWLA Press is an imprint of the Child Welfare League of America. The Child Welfare League of America is the nation's oldest and largest membership-based welfare organization. We are committed to engaging people everywhere in promoting the well-being of children, youth, and their families, and protecting every child from harm.

CHILD WELFARE LEAGUE OF AMERICA, INC.
HEADQUARTERS: 2345 Crystal Drive, Suite 250, Arlington, VA 22202

CURRENT PRINTING: 10 9 8 7 6 5 4 3 2 1

Cover and interior design by Sarah E. Barr, sarahebarr@gmail.com

Photos by Kristin Ulfsparre: Front cover and pages X, XI, 7, 8, 11, 12, 13, 14, 17, 18, 21, 22, 25, 26, 35, 36, 43, 44

Photos Courtesy of the Albany (N.Y.) *Times Union*: pages 6 (newspaper photo) and 97, and select images on hardcover casing.

Loteria Card Image (pages 87 & 88): Courtesy of the San Antonio Museum of Art, purchased with funds provided by the Folk Art Acquisition Fund

Library of Congress Cataloging-in-Publication Data

Danzig, Robert J., 1932-
  Conversations with Bobby : from foster child to corporate executive /
Bob Danzig.
     p. cm.
  ISBN-13: 978-1-58760-108-8 (hardcover)
  1. Danzig, Robert J., 1932---Childhood and youth. 2. Foster
children--United States--Biography. 3. Success--Psychological aspects.
I. Title.
  HV881.D36 2007
  362.73'3092--dc22
  [B]
                              2007014228

Printed in the United States of America

contents

Every foster child is caught in circumstances he/she did not create and cannot change—alone. Each foster child deserves an opportunity to learn how to "plow through" the pain, let that pain become secondary, and be helped to choose wisely.

Every foster child—indeed, every child—should hear the constant echo in his or her mind's eye: "You Are Worthwhile. You Are Full of Promise."

chapter 1

A DAY OF DOORS

On a cold Monday morning in January 1978, I left the Essex House Hotel in New York City and began my five-block walk to Hearst Headquarters on 57th Street and Eighth Avenue. The Central Park-facing hotel was my temporary residence while I house hunted for a permanent home for my family.

The previous Friday I closed the door to the office I had occupied for seven years as publisher of the (Albany, N.Y.) *Times Union*. I had walked the entire building—opening and closing department doors as I made a final round of handshaking and hugs of farewell to the colleagues with whom I had worked for twenty-seven years.

I had entered the *Times Union* as an office boy and through the next twenty years worked my way toward the publisher's position. I had opened and closed a lot of doors in those years. The last door I closed as I walked away was to the plant I had opened in 1970, when it became the *Times Union's* new home.

I pictured all those doors as I walked toward Eighth Avenue. When I approached Hearst Headquarters, I noticed the massive bronze framed doors majestically centered in the art deco building, with massive gargoyle statues on each corner of the exterior—silent sentries since 1932.

I stood there, stranded in a slow-motion movie. While everything around me moved at real-time paces, my world had slowed down. I noticed the lingering fog in front of my face, from my breath meeting the cool air, and was overwhelmed by a sense of melancholy.

I stared at those bronze doors, with their invitation to step inside and begin the final chapter in my newspaper career. I was the new CEO of the Hearst Newspaper Group and vice president of the Hearst Corporation, responsible for all Hearst newspapers nationwide.

I mentally compared those privileges and joys of the doors in my career to the many doors of uncertainty, disappointment, repudiation, and emotional scars that opened and closed during my childhood in a series of foster homes. I could recall no door in the blur of multiple foster home doors that was welcoming, warm, embracing, and hinting of promise for a better tomorrow.

Beginning at age two and continuing through age sixteen, the doors of my childhood represented entrances to spirit prisons. As I walked through the many doors in the series of foster homes, a portion of my spirit was locked away.

It wasn't until I graduated from high school and left the foster care system, and first joined the Hearst Newspaper Group as an office boy at the *Times Union*, that I had the opportunity to choose the doors I would open and close—doors that offered opportunity and growth.

Those early childhood doors had so many limitations. The doors I faced as a child were a stark contrast to the doors I faced that January morning, which offered an adult promise of achievement and opportunity. I was confused, emotionally bruised, unable to understand my life's direction during my younger years.

It has taken almost thirty years from that day in front of the Hearst Corporation building to find the courage to re-enter the spirit prisons behind the dark doors of my childhood. *Conversations with Bobby* is my reflection on how my childhood experiences in the foster care system became nuggets of instructions by which I would lead the rest of my life.

I crossed Eighth Avenue, with an open mind and heart, ready to face the promise and challenge ahead. I pushed that corporate bronze door open, stepped into the handsome lobby, and took the elevator to the floor where I opened the door of my new office. At that moment, I began my deeply rewarding twenty-year chapter as national CEO of the Hearst Newspaper Group.

I now realize, that when I walked through those doors, the lessons of a young, bruised, and sad foster child became a priceless possession. Although I had tried to forget him, that child still lived within me. It took writing this book to realize how often that child—Bobby—spoke to me during my Hearst career, and how often I leaned on Bobby's earlier experiences when I faced adversity. I had tried to closet Bobby, but he had never gone away. He was always there to remind me of where I came from and how important it was to remember the lessons of my youth.

conversations with bobby

chapter 2

THE CONVERSATION BEGINS

It was long after dawn and yet night refused to leave. Though the light was stifled, morning left its breath upon all that its rays should have touched. The heavy fog challenged the bulky darkness, and I remained still on the park bench, scared to disrupt the conflict. Dampness rested next to me and together we looked out at a seemingly deserted park.

Draping clouds ushered in a warm stickiness that sat upon my black slacks and loafers like thick syrup. I bent down to wipe the maple droplets from my shoe, and, in that motion, saw a black figure in the misty distance. It moved toward me, its hulking human form slowly becoming visible. Yet, the nearer it drew, the more golden in hue the hair and face grew. The closer it came, the smaller the body shrank. I could see that, what from far away appeared an aged man, was really just a small child. The boy walked toward my bench, unaware of the mystifying morning. With his head bowed, he dragged a small bag behind him. The sack lapped up the syrupy dew, leaving a clear impression in the grass of where he had been.

When he finally approached my bench, it seemed as though dampness greeted him before I had the chance, for his moist, light hair stuck to his forehead.

Looking up at me he asked, *"May I sit here, mister?"*

As I stared into his eyes, I saw something familiar. Perhaps I caught dawn's confusion, but I felt as if I knew the boy well, too well, though we had never spoken before.

"Um, mister?"

"Sure, sure, of course. Sure, sit down, sit down." I tried to give the bench a quick brush with my hand, but the boy didn't want to wait. He looked tired and frail and thankful to have a place to sit. "You're out early, son. Where are you off to in this fog?"

"Nowhere." His voice, almost inaudible, whispered in the mist.

"Well where did you come from?"

"Nowhere."

"Everyone has to come from somewhere and is going someplace. What about your folks? Where are they?"

"Nowhere."

I felt as if his seemingly simple answers were more complex than childish timidity. We sat in silence until I could think of a question that would render a different response. "What's your name, kid?"

"Bobby."

"Good name."

"What's yours?" he asked, squinting up at me.

"Bob, but I was called Bobby, too, when I was your age. How old are you?"

"Nine and a half."

"So what brings you here, Bobby, to the park?"

"I dunno. I was just walking n' I thought I heard someone calling my name. Was it you?"

I was stunned. I didn't think I had spoken aloud. "What do you mean someone was calling your name?"

"Like they were looking for me. Was it you?"

My breath became shallow. I had been thinking . . . right before the boy arrived . . . about how I couldn't remember. Could it be me that I called? No. Granted, it was true that I couldn't remember my childhood . . . but it was the weird morning; it was a delusion-inducing morning. Prior to age sixteen, I had little or no recollection . . . and I wanted to know, wanted to remember who I was . . . but it had to be the fog; it was a delusion-inducing fog. Could it be true? No. Who would believe it?

"Called you out loud?" I asked.

"Yeah, I heard it. Did you say my name?"

I shoved down so many memories during those years . . . nine and a half, in the midst of my foster shuffle . . . could I have called? The boy's parents were nowhere, he came from nowhere, he was headed off to nowhere. No, not nowhere . . . to me, he was headed to

Central Park, to my bench, to sit beside me. Before the kid showed up, I desired to recall where I came from, what I took with me, what I left behind . . . I wanted to remember the years they called me Bobby. I guess, maybe, I had called him . . . called me . . . called myself back into existence.

"Was it you, Bob? Did you call for me?"

"Yeah, I think . . . I think I did."

For the first time the boy smiled at me. "Nice to meet you Bob."

"Good to see you again Bobby."

chapter 3

FAIR TREATMENT

It was a crisp November day. Rustic-tinted leaves formed surging, muted rainbows, and a stinging breeze muffled any inner warmth extracted from the sight. I could feel a chill in my bones.

The smacking wind burnt my face, yet it was on Bobby's cheeks that I saw the reddening imprint. The boy attempted to bury his scarlet features in a jacket too small for his body. In the attempt, a shortening sleeve exposed more than a quarter of his arm. With his shoulders slouched, Bobby seemed reduced to a heap of small body parts. I wanted to protect him from the outside forces that pushed against his uncovered skin, but he seemed distant and cold.

The day before, I sat at work, mystified when I realized only a few short months ago I was Bobbyless. Yet, I couldn't really remember being without the boy. He had become a fixture in my life—like the park and the benches and the lawn bowlers and the stragglers. Bobby seemed forever in my past, but was only a short reality of my present. Our conversations constantly stewed in my brain—words, places, and faces haunted my thoughts. I drew connections frequently between his words and my actions, between what was then and the present. The boy told me about who I was and where I had been.

In response to my continual prodding from a gnawing desire to know my past, Bobby spoke about what I had endured. But that quarter of an arm exposed to the cold and that heap of small body parts sitting on the bench, showed me what I had lacked as a kid. The boy, in his physical manifestation to my eyes, spoke louder than words.

"Eleven." Bobby finally spoke. His words were visibly escaping his mouth in white staccato puffs.

"Eleven?" I questioned.

"Eleven pieces of wood in this bench."

"You counted?"

"Yes, sir. Eleven."

"What? These slats here?" I ran my hand over the seat of the bench in the same area that Bobby, just seconds ago, had been so engrossed.

The boy pointed to a single plank of wood. "Eleven of these."

"So you've said. I presume then you are good at your arithmetic."

"I've always been a good counter. Counting since I was a kid."

I chuckled at this statement while observing his small stature; it was more boy than man. But I knew Bobby's declaration had some truth to it. His demeanor was more aged than his appearance revealed. He seemed an old soul with a fresh, pink face.

"So you like mathematics then—in school, that is."

"I like to count, that's all. It helps me."

"It helps you? With your studies?"

Bobby's face wrinkled with perplexity. "No, it just helps everyday."

"Helps you with what?" I just couldn't put it together. I didn't understand.

"Helps me to run away when I have nowhere to go. Helps me pass the time."

"Counting does this for you?"

"Yes, sir. When I count, I forget things. I forget where I am—when I'm scared or all alone. When I count, I know that each minute will pass quicker. I don't feel frozen, like staring at the clock in the back of the classroom and wondering why there is always five minutes left of class. Counting makes those five minutes go away. I look at the clock, and then count to one hundred six times. I count when I breathe in and then count when I breath out and then class is over—or whatever I'm doing goes by faster."

"But why counting? How did that come about?"

"When I was scared and alone."

"When was that?" I knew, now, that I had to pry.

"A lot."

"But what started it Bobby? When was the first day you started counting?" I couldn't tell if the child wanted to talk about it or not. But, I wanted, no needed, to know. That gnawing interest in my past plagued me. I could envision the boy counting, but what for? What drove him to pick up this hobby? Who was he escaping from? Why did he want to forget things?

"In my bedroom at a foster home. They left me all alone up there. I was afraid a lot. So I counted the slats in the attic roof. It was the only thing that helped." He tilted his head back as if to count the slats; in the afternoon air they were replaced with thin bands of clouds.

I was stunned. An attic child? Don't things like that only happen in the movies—stuck with the slats in the attic. I didn't want to believe him, but that cold, quarter of an arm caught my eye again, and in that instant, the attic seemed possible.

"I didn't like the attic much," Bobby continued.

"No I'd imagine not many people would."

"The foster family didn't like it up there either. None of them ever came up. They liked to send me up there, but no one ever came with me. Not even to see if I was ok up there in the dark or if I liked my food."

"If you liked your food?"

"Well to see if I liked dinner. They left all my meals at the bottom of the attic stairs. I had to eat it up in that dark place. They were the worst meals of my life."

"I can see why."

"When I was in trouble, I was sent to my room during the day and sometimes at an early bedtime. Nighttime was scary, but daytime was lonely. I counted a lot in the day. I felt like I was always in that room." Bobby had lost the staunch. This observation brought with it a warm breeze.

"Were you ever in the rest of the house?"

"Yes, sir. I had my chores to do in the house. I had to mop the floor in the sisters' room, shine the father's shoes, fold some clothes for the mother." He was using his fingers to list the items as if each finger was reserved for a particular task. "Everyone needed me to do something for them. I did it. But I'd still get in trouble. The sisters would tell on me for things I never did." Bobby's voice rose. "They were definitely afraid of me because they would run away and cry to the mother when they saw me coming. Then I'd be counting upstairs again before I knew it."

"That sounds so cruel."

 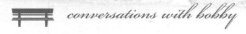

"They didn't like me. They never asked me to play with them or walk with them to school. They never took me anywhere." Bobby accelerated the speed of his words. "Not to town, nothing. No one in the family ever even said thank you or please when they asked me to do something. I just had to do it. They didn't pay me any attention until my teacher found me by the trash bins before school."

I could feel the knot in my stomach harden as I listened to Bobby.

"That's where I went when I ran away. I didn't know any other place. I only knew where the school was. I couldn't stay in that dark attic another night. And they punished me again and sent me to my room."

"When, Bobby, the night you ran away?"

"Yes, sir. That night I was sent to bed early. I counted for awhile until it got dark. Then, I was looking out of the window and thinking how I wanted to be anywhere but in that room. I've always listened to my foster families and the social worker. I never did stuff like that before, but this time I had to get out. I figured that the worst thing they could do was punish me again, and since I was already always punished for things I didn't do, why not just leave?"

"So you did?"

"Yes, sir. Out the window. I . . ."

A surge of protective parenthood could not keep me quiet. "Out the window? You went out the attic window?"

"Yes, sir. It was high up, too. We lived in the second-story apartment in the two-family home. I was scared to climb out but more scared to stay in that room. So I opened the window, leaned out, grabbed a post and stepped onto the porch roof. Then I got hold of the gutter and made my way down to the other porch roof. I swung onto the first floor porch and jumped right off. Then I ran. I ran to the only other place I knew—the school a few blocks away. And the first place I thought to go was to the trash bins. It seemed to be the only place left."

"What did you do there all that time next to the garbage?"

"I was real cold. The night was just like today. So, I stayed there and thought . . . about how cold it was and about the leftovers in the bins and about how I was a leftover—and about them finding me and sending me back."

"And you were not found until the following morning?"

"My teacher found me by the garbage. Before I knew it they were calling the social worker and my foster family. Everything happened so fast after that. The social worker saw my attic room and took me away from that family."

"Bobby, if you were sad and scared at the foster house, why didn't you just tell someone instead of running away?"

"I don't know. I guess I didn't think anyone would care." Bobby's undersized jacket and exposed skin, his small garbage bag of belongings and his need to count confirmed for the boy that he was alone in the world. "I still see and smell that dark attic, and can still remember being afraid as I climbed out on that roof."

I could feel the desperation in Bobby's story: desperate to be a part of something, desperate to be loved, desperate to be wanted and cared for like a child should. As cold as the day was that pressed upon Bobby, it did not freeze his heart. In the boy's story I felt the warmth of his rainbow muted by years of chilly isolation. "But now, son," I continued, "I know that people do care. And more importantly, I know that I care. Not only do I care about myself—mind, body, and spirit—but I care about friends and strangers alike."

LEARNING FROM THE CHILD WITHIN

Following my entry-level job as office boy at the *Times Union*, I was promoted to counter clerk in the classified advertising department. My duties included working with the customers who came personally to the newspaper ad counter to place classified ads.

Most often the ads were job-wanted and help-wanted ads. These customers were usually assigned a mailbox number by the newspaper. Ad responses were placed in the corresponding box number. Thus, there was a regular parade of such folks coming by the counter to check for replies to their job-wanted ads.

I remember observing how often the job-wanted individuals seemed discouraged and lonely, with a certain quiet desperation as they showed up hoping to find a reply—a lead in their box with a job prospect. They'd approach the box, like a child approaching a cookie jar—quietly, as if they were doing something that perhaps was wrong or undeserved. However, there were no cookies in the boxes. In most cases, there were also no replies.

As the job-wanted individuals leaned over, trying to see if perhaps a lead was pushed back, in the far corner of the box, I could sense the disdainful attitude of my co-workers when they had to occasionally serve these customers. Many of the job-wanted folks would sigh and shut the door. Some would stare at the box, others would turn around and walk away, and others would open the box again, just to do a double check.

I remember thinking "these folks are being sent to the attic" by my newspaper colleagues. They were being judged mostly because they were out of work and only able to advertise by paying cash in advance.

Over time, I took note of the customers who repeatedly bought these types of ads—often without receiving even one job lead in return. I also took note of the advertisers offering jobs in the classified ad section.

One morning I went to the office early and spread out all the job-wanted ads. I then turned to the help-wanted ads and took note of everyone who seemed a fit for one of the help-wanted ads. I mailed a copy of the corresponding job-wanted ads to the help-wanted companies.

The job-wanted regulars became a trickle. I began to automatically match any new job-wanted ad to a potential help-wanted ad every time an out-of-work customer showed up at my counter. The image in my mind as I did that matching was of the helping hand of the social worker who took me out of the attic and placed me in a more appropriate and comfortable foster home.

Years later, I found myself doing much of the same job matching, but this time it also involved preserving jobs within the Hearst Newspaper Group. Following the collapse of the economy in the early 1990s, my colleagues and I believed that when the war ended, the economy would improve and our advertising revenues would bounce back. We were wrong.

We were facing a company-wide shortfall in expected earnings. The corporate CEO advised the CEOs in charge of the different business groups that he saw no choice but to trim cost by slimming employment and reducing all other costs.

As the CEO in charge of the Hearst Newspaper Group, I told our corporate CEO that I had a deep reservation about cutting newspaper jobs. We had worked several years to create a climate of high spirit and creative talent. Those working with the newspapers had been given an opportunity to grow and let their talents flow. Job cuts, I argued, would create an atmosphere of uncertainty and insecurity. Such an atmosphere would hinder those working with us, and turn away those we might want to have join us. A loss of talent would harm, rather than help, the financial performance.

I wanted to have some time to search for a better solution. However, I had no real clue as to how to achieve this. Soon after, I read about Rick Wagoner of General Motors being promoted to North America CEO. I sent congratulatory flowers to his wife, complimenting her on the good news for her Rick. The next day I received a call from Rick's office, inviting me to attend the GM productivity sessions set for the next week.

My colleague and I spent two days absorbing GM's several programs for enhanced productivity. We returned, framed a fresh productivity program for our newspaper company, brought all of our publishers together to review the plan, and created local productivity councils at each newspaper.

We challenged the way we did business, seeking greater and more productive alternatives, rather than job cuts. We analyzed turnover, expected retirements, normal attrition. We sought out areas where the nature of the work could be changed. We looked for people we could retrain and shift from jobs we no longer needed, to jobs which needed new personnel.

Programs were identified and shared with each newspaper property until we had a new productivity program underway throughout the nation.

Developing this program took more time than laying off people. But we soon had payroll and other savings of much larger economic impact than the layoffs would have generated. We preserved our culture of talent. Throughout this period, we were fully open with our employees. As the financial performance improved, positive energy flowed from the collective achievement.

Most important of all, the Hearst Newspaper Group strengthened as a family. Those years without such ties taught me the importance of preserving relationships and helping others whenever possible. And that small role as a ringleader came in handy, as that period was much like a three-ringed circus, with so many activities going on at one time. Except this time I was a member of a family—and did it without a top hat!

Between the Lines

We often meet people who have been unfairly judged as unworthy. When that happens, we have a choice to either also shun them or we can use compassion and creativity to extend to them the same fair treatment we would like to have for ourselves.

chapter 4

A NEW-SHOES OUTLOOK

I forgot my umbrella at home. I thought the weatherman had said clouds with a chance of sunshine later in the day. Perhaps that was tomorrow's forecast. As I made my way to the park, it was drizzling steadily. I decided to take my usual walk when in my comfortably dry office, but now I wondered if I would regret the decision. Despite the doubts, I kept walking.

From far away I saw the outline of a boy standing at the edge of the park's lake. As I made my way closer, the usual grey corduroy slacks and faded navy blue shirt told me that the boy was Bobby. His clothes hugged his rounded, slouched shoulders and thin waist. He stood there with his hands in his pockets, head bowed to the water. I noticed a small hole in the back of his shirt as I came up behind him.

"What are you looking at Bobby?" I asked.

"The way the rain makes ripples on my face in the water." He said this solemnly, not as a boy fascinated by the activity.

"Ah, I see that." I stood beside him and also stared into the lake. The ripples blended our reflections together so that the peach color of my skin was touched by the youthful blush of Bobby's.

"Do you know what this reminds me of?" Bobby asked.

"Oh, I don't know. Going fishing?"

"No. No one ever took me fishing before."

"Oh. Well then, umm, going to the beach."

"No. No one ever took me to the beach before."

"Oh. I'm not sure then. What does this remind you of?"

"Shoes," Bobby replied. I started to laugh, but caught sight of his serious face between the water's ripples. Immediately I choked my laughter away.

"Shoes? How so?"

"I remember looking into people's shiny black shoes and seeing my face in them. I never had shiny black shoes." Bobby said.

I looked down to see what he wore on his feet: black scuffed-up, lackluster sneakers.

"Mind if I ask you how long you've had those sneakers for?"

"Forever." The boy replied.

"Forever is a long time. Wouldn't you have grown out of them by now?" The rain moved from a drizzle to a strong shower.

"No. They bought them for me extra big. The foster mom I lived with showed me how to crinkle up tissues and push them tight into the front of the sneaker. She told me that as my feet grew, I would need less tissues and could take some out. So sometimes I'd check to see if I was growing by pulling out the tissues from each sneaker, remove a few, crinkle the rest, and fill the toe back up."

I realized the foolishness of my question. The boy did not grow out of the sneakers, he grew into them.

"That's how I knew I was growing," Bobby continued, "as the sneaker space shrunk, I knew I was getting bigger. Only problem was that nothing else in my life grew. My school awards didn't grow, so I don't think my mind grew much. My baseball card collection didn't grow, cause I never had one card to start with. My friends didn't grow, cause I never stayed anywhere longer enough to see anyone. All I have to show are these sneakers. And I don't even like them. Whenever I look at them I think about how they are all scuffed up . . . just like me, just like I'm scuffed up. No shine on my shoes. No shine on me."

I didn't know how to respond. I thought maybe I should offer him some hope. I thought that was what he needed most, though I'm sure the boy would have preferred a new pair of shiny shoes. "When I was younger," I began, "I had a job at a fruit and vegetable store that paid me a weekly pay check. Well, I would take some of my money and set it aside each week. One day I had saved enough to make my first real purchase. And do you know what I bought?"

"Shoes?" Bobby's eyes widened.

"Yes, but not just any old shoes. I bought myself a pair of mahogany-colored Cordovan shoes. And let me tell you, Bobby, they did shine. And I loved it. I would polish them all the time, and when I walked I would frequently look down to see them glisten."

The rain came down so hard that we were forced to speak above its roar.

"What about clothes?" Bobby yelled out.

"What about them?"

"Did you ever buy any new ones? Any nice ones? All I have is this." Bobby peeled his wet navy shirt from his chest. "And I have a tan shirt, too. I have a pair of black jeans besides these grey ones."

The boy pulled at his pant leg. "I have two sets of underwear and two pairs of socks. I alternate outfits everyday. I've been wearing this for as long as I can remember. I grow into the clothes like the shoes."

"Just two?" I hollered.

"Just two. Whenever I move to another foster home, I reach under the mattress and pull out my folded black trash bag. I place my clothes in the bag and then move to a new home. I always feel ashamed at school to wear the same clothes. All the kids have clean, unwrinkled clothes. They look like someone cares about them. I never have that. I want someone to care about me."

I listened carefully to Bobby. Leaning over the water's edge I saw both our reflections in the calm surface and shared my thoughts with him.

LEARNING FROM THE CHILD WITHIN

After I started working at the *Times Union*, I started buying one nice, even elegant item of clothing every payday. At first, I saved for a quality shirt, then a lovely cashmere sweater, then a pair of Italian slacks. I cared for them, always hung them neatly or folded them carefully. I never bought or wore blue jeans or dungarees. They brought back too many memories of my childhood years.

The first time I wore a necktie to work, one of the display advertising senior salesmen, Ray DePaul, took me aside and demonstrated how to properly tie a necktie, so the dimple is perfectly centered.

Manny Kripps was someone else at the *Times Union*, whose attire was always admired. He was a very distinguished and energetic person who

overwhelmed his customers with service. He harbored an extraordinary dedication to excellence. He dressed with excellence, carried himself with excellence, and treated his customers with excellence.

I was just a young classified advertising salesman when he took me under his wing. One morning a week I'd go out with him. He always told me, "Your job is to watch the way we deal with our people; watch why it is important to give complete service to each customer."

Manny spent his entire life as a classified advertising salesman. He tackled this relatively modest work every day and always chose to excel because that characteristic was inherent in his person. "No matter what you do, be the best." He'd say. He struck a chord in me and showed me how to tune into excellence.

Between the Lines

Choose quality in all that represents you. Learn to reflect your outlook—be a shining source of strength for yourself and the others you are privileged to influence.

chapter 5

HEARTS DO MORE THAN BEAT

I watched from my bench as two boys played with sticks. Their jackets were heavier than the weather demanded, and made movement difficult for both kids. I guesstimated their age to be around six; the fact that their small hands could only carry four branches each led me to this conclusion. Their movements were wild with excitement, but showed a certain child-like focus in the intensity, as if time were suspended.

The blonde-haired boy brought his branches to the pile, where the red-headed kid waited with his branches in hand. Both dumped their sticks to the ground in blissful unison and skipped off to collect some more. Their activity made me wonder about boyhood adventures. Did their success really differ from adulthood quests?

When I looked to my right I saw Bobby sitting with me on the bench. I jolted, startled by his presence.

"Sorry Bob, didn't mean to scare you."

"Oh it's ok, Bobby, I just didn't hear you sit down."

"What are you doing?"

"Just watching these boys gathering branches, wondering what they're going to build with them. Or what game they will play."

"Maybe tic-tac-toe," the kid offered.

"Perhaps." After some silence, I spoke. "Do you play that with your friends?"

Bobby appeared hesitant. He seemed to shrink in size for a short moment as he shivered away an unwanted thought. "The real ones?" he asked as his reddening cheeks exposed an embarrassing question Bobby wished he could withdraw.

My chuckling barely allowed the words to escape, "Sure, the real ones."

"Well there weren't many real ones, Bob." There seemed a very slight indignation to his voice, perhaps a warranted reaction to my laughter.

"So you made them up?" I asked. A smile on my lips lingered in the wake of my previous laughter.

"I was forced to. I had no choice, really." This time he shrunk in resignation as the unwanted thought became audible.

The bright sun caused me to see my reflection, grin and all, in Bobby's somber eyes. The inappropriateness of my jollity stung, and my tone quickly mirrored Bobby's serious expression. "I'm sorry Bobby. I didn't mean to laugh."

"I hated Valentine's Day," Bobby said as he jumped off the bench and started kicking a rock near the bench.

I watched him flick the small rock up with the toe of his shoe, similar to soccer players with a soccer ball. He was so focused on the rock, but his comment asked for a reaction. "Why Valentine's Day, Bobby?"

"Every Valentine's Day at school kids brought cards to class and piled them up on the teacher's desk. At lunch, the teacher would go through the cards, calling the names on the front of the cards. Each time a name was called a kid would jump up and then go get the card from the teacher. Everyone always laughed and smiled."

Bobby had stopped kicking the rock and was standing in front of me. We were almost eye to eye as I sat on the bench. "I was always the new kid, so no one ever gave me a card," Bobby said, looking right into my eyes, before turning around to start kicking the rock again.

I remembered my own five children on Valentine's Day. It was always so exciting for them—preparing their cards the night before and then returning home from school the next day with the cards and candy collected that day.

Bobby circled the bench with the rock until he was behind me. "I used to buy cards for myself and sign other kids' names on them and put them on the teacher's desk so that I wasn't the only one without cards."

Bobby's voice was behind me, but the memory was in front of me. Painful. I didn't know what to say. Bobby continued, "I carried those cards from foster home to foster home in my black plastic trash bag. I pulled the cards out and sometimes forgot that I had signed the names. I finally buried them all in the back of a neighborhood fire station in Watervliet, New York. It was a card cemetery. I wanted to visit the cards, but I didn't want to see the other kids' names signed in my handwriting anymore."

Bobby had circled back to the front of the bench. He stopped kicking the rock and joined me on the bench. We both watched the two boys in front of us playing with sticks. I looked at Bobby and wondered what he was thinking. My heart was breaking. I reached over and patted his small shoulder. He looked up at me and smiled—not full grin, but more of a slight grin, paired with sad eyes.

$$\mathcal{Cee}$$

Learning from the Child Within

In 1964 a group of colleagues walked out on contract bargaining and chose to strike instead.

The other unions each had labor agreements, honored them, and came to work each day. Volunteers came to the plant each day to help produce the newspaper. And each day the newspaper continued to come out, the striking union members became more bitter, loud, irrational, and frightened. They were scared that the unnecessary strike might result in loss of jobs for the hundreds of strikers.

When the strike was settled a few weeks later and management permitted the strikers to return to their jobs, the minds and hearts of many of the executive managers were hurting, disappointed, and unconsciously tilted toward retaliation.

It became apparent within a week—the employees were angry and uncertain, and their supervisors were frustrated and unforgiving.

I was personnel manager and assistant business manager for the newspaper, in a position to see the wide range of unhealthy and vindictive actions by several different department managers and the hardening employees. I knew that unhealthy pattern could set in when the heart was heavy and perceived mistreatment.

I proposed to the publisher that a cooperation committee be set up with members from each department's employee group, union reps, and rotating managers. The group would meet each week to be a place for airing claims of mistreatment. It would be a place to examine the hurt and try to heal the hearts.

The vengeful actions stopped. Employees became more concerned with making up for the lost business during the strike. In fact, the cooperation committee set a new foundation for labor relations. The union and management representatives changed over the years, but the dedication to heal hearts did not. The cooperation team had essentially written Valentine's Day cards to others in the company. They offered them the joy of being wanted and valued.

Between the Lines

Hurt hearts can look for new ways to seek out goodness in others. Those who have had hurt hearts have a personal understanding of the pain accompanying that hurt. They know that many feel a need to retaliate and hurt others in return, but they also know that the greater good is in helping others in similar pain. They have the insight and understanding needed to help others heal. Hearts beat to feed the body and heal to fuel the spirit.

chapter 6

FRAGRANCE OF FRIENDSHIP

Fall was in the air as I walked through the park that afternoon. It was cold enough to bring the heavy jackets out of the closet, but not that miserable cold, that sweeps up under your jacket, no matter how thick it is.

The sky was turning the color of the golden leaves. It was late in the afternoon, but because it was fall, the sky was already turning dark, and the sun was halfway between night and day on the horizon, creating a soft, muted, golden effect.

As I walked around the corner to my favorite bench, the smell of roasted chestnuts welcomed me. Vendors in the park were busy selling smells rather than chestnuts. The comforting scents reminded everyone to slow down, relax, and enjoy New England at its best—comforting colors in the foliage and invigorating cool breezes were the calm before the holiday hustle-and-bustle storm.

As I approached the bench, I saw Bobby waiting for me. I wasn't ready to sit with him yet, so I stopped in front of the vendor to buy chestnuts instead. I was still reliving our last conversation about his pretend friends. I had a large group of friends, a wonderful bride, five children, and a growing number of grandchildren. I didn't have the loneliness that caused Bobby so much pain.

When I turned away from the vendor, I noticed Bobby watching me. I crossed over the path, and offered him the long paper cone of chestnuts. He smiled and pulled back the tape on top as I sat down.

"The smell makes you feel good, doesn't it?" I asked.

Bobby unfolded the top of the cone and nodded yes. "It reminds me of Mrs. Davis."

"Was she one of your teachers?"

"She's Wilson's mom."

I let out a sigh as I nodded my head. Bobby had a friend.

"Wilson is the first friend I had. I can't remember a lot of the places I lived, but I always remember the home in Troy, N.Y., because it smelled like fried fat. Mrs. Wilson was always cooking."

As Bobby stopped speaking, I could see the wheels of his memory screeching to a stop and lingering on Wilson and his mom.

"You could smell dinner at breakfast. We'd come in from the snow and Mrs. Wilson would have cookies and hot chocolate ready for us. I could always smell the cookies and last night's dinner at the same time."

"Sounds like you had a good friend there."

"He was. We would do everything together. Spent most of our days together. We would walk to school together and walk home together. We would just sit on the sidewalk and talk. Sometimes we'd go around visiting, talking to Mr. Cohen, who owned the furniture store below our apartments. We would play games, go on adventures, and rescue each other from thieves and sorcerers. Then we would have one of Mrs. Davis' good smelling meals."

Bobby put his nose to the chestnuts and took in a long breath, and then leaned back, his back straight against the bench, as his head tilted up, looking at the falling leaves. "I was sad when he left."

"What happened?" I asked, concerned about the sudden turn in his story.

"It was a Saturday morning. I had almost counted all thirty stairs to Wilson's home, when I saw the orange paper on his door. I didn't know what it said, but I knew it was bad because I couldn't smell Mrs. Davis' food and there was a padlock on the door."

My heart sunk. I knew too well what the orange notice meant for the Davis family. During those years, a padlock and orange notice pointed to eviction. "Did you find out where he went?" I quietly asked as I joined Bobby in staring at the falling leaves, rather than staring at him with a broken heart.

"My foster mother told me that the sheriff made them leave because Wilson's family hadn't paid its rent."

"Did you ever see him again?"

"No. But I'll never forget him. Sometimes I walk by a restaurant and smell Mrs. Davis' cooking, but I know she's not really there."

Bobby and I looked from the sky back down at the chestnuts in his lap. He reached toward me and offered one. "They do smell good," he added.

"Yes, Bobby. That's the fragrance of friendship."

Learning from the Child Within

I remember so well my sophomore year of high school, a geometry classmate who I did not really know, Perry Crawford, and I were the only two in the classroom when I dared him to a chalk eraser battle. We threw those well-chalked erasers with all our might as we ran around the classroom.

It was pure fun until I threw the eraser near the door just as the teacher walked in. The eraser hit him square on the cheek and left both a red rash and the chalky imprint of the eraser. He furiously marched us directly to the principal's office.

Both Perry and I were suspended from school for a week. As we left the building, he asked what I would do for the week with no school. I shrugged my shoulders. I didn't know.

Perry asked if I would like to come and spend the day at his house and have dinner with his family. I wasn't happy about being suspended from school, but I was excited about having a new friend. We decided on a day and he gave me directions to take the bus to his street.

When I arrived at his house—an actual house—all brick with a welcome sign on the door, neatly tailored lawn, and a shiny black driveway, I stood looking at the house thinking I had never been in an actual house—only apartments.

Perry showed me his record collection and let me touch the saxophone he played in the school band. His father, also named Perry, was an electrician whose early shift allowed him to be home by mid-afternoon. He was sitting in what he later told me was his favorite chair, reading the afternoon newspaper. Perry's mother was in the kitchen singing softly to herself as she prepared the pot roast supper that I was invited to share. His sister, Shirley, was at the dining room table doing her homework. She was a busy college student.

conversations with bobby

It warmed me all over to see an actual family intact, peaceful, supportive, and complete. It was the first time I ever actually experienced such a complete family life. That day began a life-long friendship with Perry. We double dated, went to Sunday jazz concerts together, were both godparents for our children, and spent every New Year's Eve together.

Although our lives took different paths as we became adults and set out on our own unique career paths, we never let our careers get in the way. The Crawford family had become my model for family life. They taught me to treasure friendship for life, to treasure one's children, and to make one's home a place of peace, support, and love.

Today I have special pals who I hike with every Saturday morning, followed by a deli breakfast together. That same group of pals does isometric water walking every Sunday morning, also followed by a deli breakfast. We date as couples and enjoy those events.

At home, being a friend to my bride, and to my now-adult children, has added a special dimension to our relationships. We spend time with each other because we are friends, rather than just because we are family and feel an obligation to visit each other. We love and value our friend relationship.

Between the Lines

Perry was my first long-term friendship. He taught me to value the people I met in both my personal and private life because, in the end, friendship is a powerful relationship. At both work and home, a friendly attitude, or a developed friendship with colleagues or family members, makes harsh situations bearable, and nurtures cooperative efforts.

Friends are our counterbalances, pulling us back up to the peak when we find ourselves stuck in the valleys of our lives.

chapter 7

FAULT LINES

I could smell the rain. Mother Nature gave her not-so-subtle hint of what was coming. The park was growing dim with each passing moment. Smoky, thin clouds darkened the trees, and the wind whipped the leaves in random, sporadic rotations. The branches were twirling in ways that seemed to defy expectations of wood. The barks were grasping tightly, hoping not to lose one. Some rapid snaps indicated that a few branches just couldn't hold on.

It was a wild evening. One sensed chaos in the atmosphere. Nature's war rang on in the park.

Bobby sat beside me. His blonde hair was blowing in knotty waves. He secured his glasses onto his nose in fear he might lose them.

"Crazy night, huh Bobby?"

"Yes. Like the world got in trouble and is being punished by the wind," the boy responded.

I was impressed with his simile, or was it metaphor? I mixed up such technical labels.

"Yes, like the world got in trouble. I like that." I said.

We sat there for a few minutes as the wind rushed around us and the smell of rain became more pungent. Bobby slid down in the bench until his feet were touching the ground. He drew a square in the dirt and fixed his feet inside the square. I broke the silence by asking, "Bobby, have you ever been in trouble before?"

"I got in big trouble with a foster mom a couple years ago. She was so mad at me that she chased me around the block with a chain-linked dog leash," the boy responded.

"What happened?" With his soft demeanor and quiet disposition, I couldn't imagine the boy doing anything that would warrant such punishment.

"Well, I know now that it was my fault. But I didn't know then how wrong I was. I tried to blame my friend, Richard, but the foster mom saw through it. I think that's why she was even more mad, because I didn't take responsibility."

"Responsibility? Is that what she said?"

"She said that I didn't take responsibility for my actions. So that's why she chased me around with the leash. She said she wouldn't have used it. She promised she would never hurt me like that. But I didn't know she wouldn't have used it when it was happening. I was so scared. It was like a nightmare."

"Well what did you do wrong?"

"Well, I had a classmate named Richard who lived only a couple blocks away from the foster parents. He used to come by the house to play since he lived so close, and we became friends. One week, Richard and me and our whole class were going on a horseback-riding trip. We were going to the O'Rourke stables that had saddled horses for riding. The school told us that the O'Rourke's charged two dollars for an hour on the horses. We all had to pay for the rides ourselves.

"When Richard was over at my foster parents' house before the trip to the O'Rourke stables, he saw my foster mom's jar of quarters. Richard told me that his parents were away on a trip and that his grandmother was watching him. He said that he usually got an allowance every week, but wouldn't get one that week until after the horseback-riding trip. Richard asked if he could borrow eight of the quarters in the jar so that he could go to the O'Rourke stables and ride. I didn't have a good feeling about it. I didn't want to do it, but I did it anyway."

As I sat and listened to Bobby, I noticed that nature seemed to be a paralleled back drop for his story. As the wind picked up, so did Bobby's story. As more branches broke around us, I motioned to Bobby to stand. The night was rough, so I encouraged him to continue his story as we walked toward shelter.

"I forced the cork off of the jar. The cork was stuffed down so far that I broke it into pieces. When I finally opened it, I gave Richard the two dollars and tried to close it back up, but the cork was all broken. I left it looking as best as I could. I thought no one would notice. I was wrong.

"When we came home from the stables, later that day, the foster mom noticed the jar. She called me to the kitchen table and placed the coin jar in front of me. I knew she knew. She asked me what happened to her jar. I don't know why I didn't just tell her I broke into it. But I didn't. I said, 'Richard took it.' The foster mom didn't like that answer and asked me again what happened to it. I screamed, 'It was Richard!' And then I ran out of the house. That's when she grabbed her dog Skippy's metal leash. She ran after me. I ran across the street past the firemen sitting outside their station. She was right behind me swinging the leash above her head. The firemen cheered for her each time we passed them. When we went around the third time, I tripped right in front of everyone. The foster mom stood above me and asked, 'Who touched my jar?'

"By now I was crying and I gave up. I said that it was me who took the money out of the jar. I gave the quarters to Richard without asking permission. I took what wasn't mine. The foster mom stopped twirling her leash and sat down next to me. That's when she said those words, 'All I wanted you to do was take responsibility for your actions. I wouldn't have hit you.' I was glad it was over and never forgot that day."

"Bobby, that was a good lesson," I said as I guided him toward the Nature Observatory in Central Park's Belvedere Castle. As we went through the doors, the storm behind us, I remembered two tornado-sized messes I once made myself, and how taking responsibility proved to be my life preserver.

$$\mathcal{C}\!\ell\ell$$

Learning from the Child Within

When I first joined the advertising sales staff at the *Times Union*, Angelo Monaco (Angie to everyone) was the retail-advertising sales manager. Angie had a face that looked as if it was chiseled from a mountainside: deep lines, a permanent frown, a long oval face, all topping a reluctant shirt and necktie-framed neck.

Angie looked and acted like a "man's man." Although I rarely saw him smoke a cigarette, I never saw him without a long, black, ivory-tipped cigarette holder in his lips. It seemed more prop than habit and had the desired effect of causing one to look at his lips carefully when his low pitched voice was whispering some instruction through and around that cigarette holder. Intimidation seemed his ally against any who had a direct reporting relationship to him.

At the time, my sales territory was the grocery stores. A major account was the A&P chain, which favored our *Times Union* only slightly because we had a Sunday newspaper and our competitor did not. A&P was opening their Albany Superstore, and all the national executives were to be in

Albany for the Monday morning opening. Kick-off for the event was to be a two-page ad in our Sunday *Times Union*. I handled the account, processed the ad, and was frankly "pumped up" with pride at our coup of having the launch exclusively in our newspaper.

On Sunday morning I raced to get the paper and flipped through the pages looking for the colorful opening ads for the new superstore. No ad. Sinking feeling. Disaster looming in my imagination, I drove to the newspaper plant and talked to the composing room foreman, who then chased down the original copy. The insertion date for the ad to run, in my clear handwriting, was for the following Sunday. I had scheduled the ad for the biggest event in A&P history for the wrong Sunday.

I wandered out of the plant devastated, confused, and certain my career was over. Almost without thinking, I drove to the home of Angie Monaco, who was just returning from church with his family. I burst out in a shriek that I had incorrectly scheduled the major opening ad.

Angie leaned against the car, slowly took out his cigarette holder, managed that tight-lipped grin and said, "You cannot be telling me you left the ad out of the paper can you?"

"Yes," I answered.

With that, he waved his arm, beckoning me to follow him into the house. Once inside, he picked up the telephone and asked for the home number and address of Jack Casey, the A&P regional manager. With address in hand, he stormed out of the house, barely giving me enough time to follow, and we drove to Jack Casey's home.

Angie rang the bell, and when Jack answered, told him what I had done. They both stared at me, and then Angie said, "We are here to start over and get four pages of opening announcements in the Monday morning paper—two pages in the first section and two pages in the second section, all without charge to A&P."

Jack agreed with the remedy and the three of us set off to the newspaper to make the arrangements. On the drive down, Angie told Jack that we must keep in mind that the only reason A&P's opening day could be saved by running the double impact ads on Monday was because I had owned up, sought him out, and acted like a partner, rather than a simple employee. Jack agreed. Later that day a fruit basket arrived at my home with a message from Jack: "You Saved the Day Partner. Thank You!"

On Monday I told Angie about the basket. He smiled for the first time I could remember, and said that the life lesson for me was always to step up to the plate when a mistake had occurred. That lesson—about the importance of stepping to the plate—served me well at all levels of my career.

At the time of the Hearst Corporation's 100-year anniversary preparations in 1987, I was the CEO of the Hearst Newspaper Group and vice president of the Hearst Corporation.

Many events and activities were planned a full year in advance. Among them was the publication of a silver centennial booklet, which would celebrate the talent of the entire corporation.

A well-known graphic design agency was hired to prepare the book. They suggested that we fly our newspaper editors to New York City, where

each would be interestingly posed in a unique fashion as part of a group photograph for the centennial booklet. The photo shoot took place about a year in advance of the publication. The idea had a "buzz" to it—the exciting key component needed to celebrate 100 years of great talent.

About four months before the anniversary date, I suddenly realized that several staff changes had occurred since the photograph was taken. Some editors had retired, one had passed away, and new editors had replaced them. I called the graphic design agency. They advised me that local photographers at each newspaper could photograph the new editors and their agency would insert the replacement pictures.

My problem solved, I forgot about it and we all began firming up our other anniversary events. Without my knowing, the centennial issue went to press.

Someone at the printer producing the anniversary issue knew some of our editors and also knew someone at *Time* magazine. He tipped them off that our Hearst centennial book was printed with the heads of our newspaper editors on other people's bodies.

Time went to press with a silhouette outline of the changed photos and the group photo shoot of our centennial book. They asked readers to name the mystery editors.

Our corporate communications director, who was apoplectic as he stumbled over his words, called me to describe the *Time* article. I was numb and convinced this error could end my Hearst corporate career.

The next morning, I had a call from Frank Bennack Jr., our president and corporate CEO, asking me to bring our corporate communications director to his office. Frank had a long oval-shaped table in his conference room, with about 50 copies of *Time* magazine all opened to the offending article.

"Have you seen these?" he asked.

"Well, yes," I said, "but I haven't seen this many copies."

He looked at me straight in the eyes and asked "How could this possibly happen?"

Although I felt my career slipping away, I said, "This is my responsibility. I never checked the proofs after the graphic design agency made the changes. They simply changed the heads of our new editors and inserted them on the former editors' bodies. They took a shortcut, but I did not take the time to check. I own the problem."

The next moment is etched deeply in my psyche, he said, "In a situation like this there is only one thing to do."

I thought, "Here comes the guillotine, off goes my head."

Then he said, "The only thing to do is laugh!" When he said that, I laughed long and hard with relief. He also said to me "Thank you, Bob, for taking responsibility. Someone else would have the fault line at someone else's feet. Good for you."

Curiously, the *Time* magazine article made the silver Centennial book perhaps the most celebrated in any company's 100-year anniversary. It became a collector's item.

During another point in my career as CEO of the Hearst News Group, I took part in a purchase of a small paper, with a circulation of 20,000. The paper served a town in Texas, and about seven thousand copies a day were also distributed to the neighboring city across the border in Mexico.

A year after we purchased the paper, we discovered that the newspapers being printed and shipped to the distribution warehouse in Mexico were not being distributed to customers. The papers were sold to a recycler of newsprint and destroyed every week. In short, the advertising rates, which were based on a 20,000 audited circulation, were inflated. It was just a camouflage for a flim flam.

Facing this reality, we knew this problem was ours to handle. We owned the paper. There was nothing to gain out of suing the former owner.

Rather than changing practices and ensuring that the newspapers reached readers across the boarder, we decided to approach the advertising community, and share the reality—that a year of our ownership had gone by, when we were unwittingly overcharging the advertisers.

We calculated the cost overage for every advertiser and advised them that we were establishing an advertising bank to which we would make a deposit in the amount of their individual overcharge during the previous year. The advertisers were told that they could draw down these accounts as free advertising each month that they maintained their regular advertising schedule. Thus they would have free additional advertising to reach readers every single month.

We announced this program at a large reception for the advertising community. When they heard our story, they burst into spontaneous applause. They whistled and cheered. Privately, many told me how much they appreciated our honesty and integrity.

Although we sent repeat reminders of the ad bank available to each advertiser, not a single advertiser accessed the bank. Our honesty in handling a shame-filled incident was enough for them.

Between the Lines

When the mistake is yours, major or minor, dust particle or boulder, stand up and take responsibility. When you do, it is step one in resolving an issue and an example of the right thing to do the next time a similar invitation to err presents itself. When one's purpose is clear, the largest mistakes can often be cleared up with what in the end feels like little effort.

chapter 8

JOINING THE BIG LEAGUES

The crack of a baseball bat startled Bobby. His small shoulders jerked forward as he pressed his hands hard against the bench. "Just a game going on behind us," I said.

"I know," the boy replied. Bobby gazed into the sky. Perhaps he was watching the game unfold in his mind. Perhaps he saw himself as the batter, shocked by his first home run. I couldn't tell. I couldn't enter.

Like the crack of the bat, I wanted to break the silence. "You know, Bobby, we could play baseball sometime if you'd like. I'm not that good myself, but I'm sure we could help each other."

"No, thank you, I don't know how to play," the boy replied.

"Well we could learn together. I have a bit of know how. Not much skill, but I'm sure I could show you a thing or two."

"I can't play sports. Only the regular kids do that."

"The regular kids? You can run and jump and catch just like the rest of them."

"Sports are for normal people, Bob."

"You are normal. Come on, give it a try. You could be part of a winning team. Trust me, I know. You are a team player. With training and practice you could be cracking bats and sliding into bases." I wasn't going to let the kid get away with that attitude.

"I guess I never thought it was for me. I just never felt comfortable joining in. Besides, no one ever asked me to."

"I never felt comfortable much with sports either. I understand what you are saying, Bobby. You feel out of your element. You'd rather stay on the sidelines."

"Yeah, I think the sideline is where I should stay." He was talking to the clouds, glazed over and distracted. Perhaps he was on the sideline now, waving the batter home. Perhaps he was on the bleachers, cheering for the players. Perhaps he was in the parking lot, kicking a rock.

"But you know Bobby, you don't have to stay on the sideline. Life isn't as much fun if you're always watching. Sometimes you just have to get in the game."

Bobby opened his mouth slightly as if to speak, but nothing seemed to come out. In the wind, though, I heard a faint whisper of the words he had breathed, "I'm afraid I'll strike out."

Striking out. I remembered that feeling well.

LEARNING FROM THE CHILD WITHIN

When I was working at the *Times Union*, a few friends and I would have lunch together. We'd all talk and eat and talk some more. I remember in particular this one copy boy that would eat with us. He would always talk

about sports. He loved sports. Even wanted to be a sports reporter. And he had quite the stories to share about his cousin, Bill Mazeroski.

Bill was one of the best players in Major League Baseball. And boy did my friend let us know it everyday. Bill played for the Pittsburgh Pirates. We heard stories about this guy so often that we felt like he was our family, too. Who would have thought that this guy would play a big role in my life.

I'd been working with the *Times Union* for a number of years at this point and wanted to be considered for the retail ad manager position. Unfortunately, to my surprise, the newspaper told me that I was just too young to get the job. I was crushed. I knew I could do it. And, I knew I could do it well. But I had no way of showing them. I had no way of getting off the sidelines and into the game. Or, so I thought.

After receiving the news, I went to call on one of my clients, Frank Nigro—what a good man. He was someone I could confide in, someone that really listened. Known by family and friends as FJN, he was one of Albany's leading food merchants. He took one look at me and asked what was going on. He said I didn't seem to be my usual self.

I explained what had happened and FJN told me to resign. But I told him I couldn't—I had a wife and kids. "Resign and come work for me," was FJN's solution. "You'll become my advertising and sales promotion director for the food chain. You can also become promotion director of the shopping center I'm opening."

This was the second time FJN had suggested a change that would alter my career. About three years earlier, my colleagues and I were in direct competition with the Gannett-owned *Knickerbocker News*, which had 100 percent of Albany's food advertising market. I went to our advertising director, Mr. Mark Collins, and asked to handle the retail advertising food section.

I told Mr. Collins that I had some new ideas for the food advertising section. If he gave me a six-month trial period to manage the food section, I told him I would agree to also handle my classified job without a salary increase. If he felt I was falling down on the job, he could stop the experiment. Mr. Collins gave me the opportunity, but insisted I give up the classified territory. So, I left my old job and began a new sales position with zero business.

FJN owned the Albany Public markets, which he literally built up from a single corner outside vegetable bin. I called on FJN every day with a new idea. I would take ads from the competing *Knickerbocker News*, add a new spin and show him how much more effective they could be. I'd bring him a piece of research each and every day.

I don't think I was in the food section sixty days when FJN astonished me by splitting his advertising. Instead of running ten pages a week exclusively in the *Knickerbocker News*, he ran five pages in both newspapers. Within one year, the *Times Union* owned Albany's food advertising market. The other food retailers followed FJN's lead, creating an increasing loss of revenue for the *Knickerbocker News*. Within two years the *Times Union* acquired the *Knickerbocker News*.

When FJN asked me to work for him that day, I couldn't refuse the offer. I wanted to be in the game, so I took the job and left the newspaper. It was a hard decision, but I knew I needed to do something challenging. I needed to get out there. And that's what I did.

However, I didn't have the slightest idea what I was doing. My job was to come up with this grand plan for opening the new store. But how was I going to draw a crowd for the big opening day ceremony? As much as I wanted to be in the game, I didn't know the rules. Then it came to me. What about Bill Mazeroski? What if I could get him to come to the grand opening? Wouldn't that draw a crowd?

I knew many people would come out to meet him. He hit the winning home run in the last inning of the World Series, defeating the defending champions, the New York Yankees. He was on top of his game. But would he really show up? Would he really do it?

So, I made a phone call to my lunch buddy. I figured maybe he could help me out. And besides, because of my friend, I felt as if Bill and I were already family. So, my friend called Bill, and, what do you know, Bill said he would do it. He would be the celebrity guest at the grand opening of the shopping center. In shock and gratitude, I got to work. I developed all of the advertising around Bill. Despite knowing very little about sports, I pieced together a sports theme and spread the word.

Well, needless to say, on the day of the ceremony, people came out in droves. When I announced him to the crowd, he had me stand at the edge of the platform, as if we were on the baseball diamond, and he threw me the 'opening pitch.' I had never been picked for a team, never played a sport, always on the sidelines, yet there I was, catching a pitch from a professional baseball icon in front of a cheering audience. It was a great day, for I knew at that moment that I rose to the challenge. Not only did I play the game, but I hit a home run.

The shopping center opening was an enormous success and the *Times Union* put Bill's opening-pitch picture on the front page. And within a week, the newspaper called asking if I would still be interested in the position for which I'd been told I was too young to be given.

FJN knew before I opened my mouth that they offered me the job. He also knew how much I wanted it. He said to me, "You're supposed to be a newspaper man, so go be one. I only offered you a port in the storm until they realized their mistake in thinking you were too young for that job."

He was just giving me the chance to get in the game. He saw the potential. He saw the hidden talent. He saw that I was tired of standing on the sidelines. So, I took the job back at the newspaper. I went back confident and energized. I went back knowing that I could crack a couple bats.

Between the Lines

There are many types of teams, coaches, and players in all aspects of life. If you want to play, you have to step forward and "try out." Standing on the sidelines waiting to be picked isn't enough. You have to show others that you can play and succeed.

Bill Mazeroski didn't allow one of baseball's all-time great teams to intimidate him. He stepped to the plate and created one of baseball's greatest moments.

FJN didn't go from owning a one-bin vegetable stand to being the owner of one of the largest supermarket chains in Albany by waiting for someone to offer him an opportunity. He recognized potential and acted on opportunity whenever it appeared.

As a player and coach, you also have to be willing to offer others a "port in the storm." When FJN did that for me, it was an indelible lesson—true leaders create teams by going the extra mile for employees and colleagues.

Life has detours, disappointments, reversals for us all. The decision to sit or play—and the type of player and coach you become—is your choice. Don't sit on the sidelines. Join the big leagues and create your opportunity to succeed.

chapter 9

GRAY IS NOT A RAINBOW

Coming around the curve to the place where the willow tree branches hang over the edge of the pond, I spotted him: Man With Newspaper. That was the best I could do. My creative juices were overworked, thus, Man With Newspaper had to suffice for his identity. But he need not feel slighted, for Woman With Novel sat only a few feet away on her bench, and, without having reached the end of the pond, I already knew Grandfather With Cane and Lady With Dog were on their respective benches as well. It seemed more appropriate to name them according to their activity. I could have called Man With Newspaper, Guiseppe or Raul, but his defining characteristic was found in his *New York Times*. So I justified my lack of creativity in this area and adopted the three-name label for all of the regulars.

I took comfort in passing them on my walks through the park. Though we never spoke, I saw many of them more often than I saw close friends. A simple nod was all that was necessary, a mutual glance recognizing shared space, shared regularity, like one tree smiling to another. The familiar strangers of Central Park had become part of the landscape.

Of course, I, too, took my place in the landscape. An imaginary reserved sign rested on my bench by the lawn bowlers. Only one other person in the world had the courage to sit beside me: Bobby. For years I had sat alone, but for the past several months, I had shared my bench with the boy in exchange for enlightenment of the past. Sometimes we talked about everything, sometimes about meaningless nothing.

Today I couldn't stop wondering about those regular faces in the park. Unintentionally, I spoke the words I was thinking out loud. "You know Bobby, at another time of the day, there are different regulars here in the park, someone else's familiar strangers. And those people will nod at each other and find comfort in each other."

"What are you talking about, Bob?"

"These people, on the benches. Look, over there, Guy With Radio, he is my regular. He is here at this time everyday. He sits there and watches the lawn bowlers like I do, just from a different angle. He's got his bench, I've got mine. I can depend on seeing him. But other people, at other times of the day, they have their regulars. Maybe in a few hours that bench will be someone's Fellow With *Newsweek* or Girl With Doll. A new set of familiar strangers will replace us. There will be new fixtures here, and people will depend on seeing those usual faces."

"I don't understand. I never really noticed that guy until just now. All I see today is a gray day—cloudy and gray," replied Bobby.

"But what about Grandfather With Cane, did you not see him on your way here? Or Lady With Dog? Didn't you notice the chocolate lab?"

"No, I would have noticed chocolate on my way. Really, I would. I don't know what you mean. All I see today is that everyone looks gray—the park looks gray, the people look gray, the trees look gray. The whole world is gray. Haven't you noticed that today, Bob? Haven't you noticed the big clouds? Haven't you noticed that there is no color?"

To tell the truth, I hadn't really noticed the impending storm. I was too distracted by the thought of the familiar strangers that I neglected to note the weather. But the kid was right; the day sure was shadowed. It was as if we were cast in a black and white film, with only hues of gray available to showcase life. I wanted to continue my explanation of the significance of Fellow With *Newsweek* or Girl With Doll, but I could see that Bobby wasn't interested. The color of this cloudy day overshadowed Bobby's thoughts, leaving him unable to focus upon any other topic. The boy was too preoccupied by the muted landscape.

"No," I said, "I haven't noticed the clouds. But now that you mention it, I guess it is kind of gray looking out here."

"Well I don't know how you didn't see that there was no color. Look at the branches and the water and the ground and the sky. It's all gray. It's like everything is dead. And Radio Guy over there has no color either. Are you sure he's even alive?"

A simple observance from a kid—the gray sky casting down a bleak tinge—turned into an intriguing question. Granted, the park appeared as Bobby described: a thickly clouded winter sky mirrored its colors down onto the earth and its inhabitants. But the question . . . that was something to be pondered. Could these familiar strangers be likened to ghosts sitting in their bench pews? Was each pew their burial plot and they themselves, a living headstone? One must admit, the park regulars were like cemetery residents: random strangers buried beside each other, destined to be silent neighbors. It was an eerie thought that enhanced the grayness of the day. Or perhaps the grayness of the day beckoned such eerie thoughts.

"Radio Guy might not be alive?!" Bobby seemed to mistake my silence for lack of surety.

"Of course he's alive," I finally replied. "He's here everyday. It is the day he doesn't come to the park that the question might be more appropriate."

"You know Bob," the boy's words lingered in his mouth as he sighed deeply, "I don't know."

"You don't know what?"

"I don't know what you're talking about. I don't know much, really."

The quick change of subject rattled my thoughts. I wanted to continue musing upon the regulars and their new gray-ghost tint, but I knew I should further whatever was on Bobby's mind. I cherished his thoughts; it was a way to understand from where he came. It was a way to understand from where I came.

"What do you mean you don't know much? You know a lot, son. You are a very bright and articulate boy."

"I don't know decimals. We're supposed to know that for school, and I know nothing about it. Any of it. I think you're supposed to line them up somehow, but I don't know where or for what. What's a tens? What's a ones?"

"I'm not quite sure I know what you're talking about either. But what does decimals have to do with anything?"

"I don't know how to sentence structure. We're supposed to know that, too, for school. I passed the grade. I dunno how. Verbage and Nounage? I don't know what they are."

"Verbage and Nounage?"

"I don't know fractions either. They're the worst. I've had to pretend with them forever."

"Fractions? Where is this coming from?"

"From my teachers. They are always fracturing."

"No, I mean, where is this lack of confidence in your studies coming from?"

Bobby was beyond listening. "I don't know what to do, so I just try to disappear. I just pretend I am lining up the decimals. I pretend to pick out the verbage and fraction my numbers. And it works. But I don't know any of it. I can't think in class."

"Well why not just start paying attention more to the teacher? Or ask her for help with the work?"

"I can't be trouble. I can't be trouble for anyone . . . not the teacher, not my foster family."

Like the landscape, I thought, like the landscape. Bobby wanted to blend in, to be a part of the landscape of the classroom. He didn't want the teachers to notice his lack of understanding because that would cause trouble. But what did "trouble" really mean for the boy? Did it mean he would be moved to a new home, only to have to begin again at another school and another family with new sets of rules? How could the child expect to learn if he always had to adjust? His life was like a waterfall, always moving water, never to be set in place.

"I was afraid they were going to move me out again," Bobby continued. "I was worried about the coal I had to carry, that's why my fractions are still all wrong."

"The coal?"

"Yes, sir. The year we learned fractions I had moved in with a new family. The foster mother had a severe limp, with one leg much shorter than the other leg, and she had two sons that were older than me. They had a big coal stove in the kitchen and a smaller stove in the front room. The coal bin was in the basement and they told me I had to bring the coal up twice a day. I'd lift the bucket of coal a step, set it down and take a breath, and then lift it to the next step and take another step. That's how I made it—before school and then first thing after school. I didn't think I could make it to school after I brought that bucket up all those stairs, but I knew I had to."

"So you've said. Why didn't you tell your family it was too much?"

"I didn't want to leave. Besides, it was my job. They said so. And they let me live with them so I had to. I wanted to help. But the coal was so far down. So many stairs and so heavy and so dark. I shoveled, but I didn't want to. I carried too, but I didn't like it. At school I thought about having to do it all again when I got home. But at school I was supposed to be fractioning and verbage and subjectors. And so I pretended all the time. I was so scared of the basement and it was so heavy. That's all I could think about."

The more Bobby released his memories, the more I drew the connection: he had become as gray as the day. Any spark of color would attract attention to his growing fears and diminished understanding of reading, writing, and arithmetic. Not only was he part of the landscape within his classroom, equivalent to the desks and chalkboard, but he also desired to be shadowed. He viewed life in hues of gray, and preferred others to view him in the same color scheme. In this way, he merely existed.

Bobby continued, "I was so afraid they were going to get rid of me. So I carried the coal every day. Twice a day. Because everyone always got rid of me. I couldn't do decimals and think about them taking me away again. I was always moving and always thinking about my next place. By the time I got settled, I was moved. So verbage wasn't easy for me. Neither was subjectoring or fractions. So now I don't know."

Back to the beginning. He doesn't know. "I think you know more than you give yourself credit for," I replied.

"No, I didn't notice Radio Guy or The Doggie Lady. I didn't notice the chocolate. I don't know much, really."

"So, it's ok that you didn't notice Guy With Radio or any of the others. I was just rambling before, really. It's just something I happened to have picked up over the years. I like to watch people, and I like the security in seeing a familiar face. Maybe I like it because I didn't see many regular faces in my lifetime. Maybe that's why I noticed."

"Nothing about my life is regular. And I'd rather not be noticed," Bobby stated.

"Did I ever tell you that I graduated college?" I asked

"No."

"Well I did. But I wasn't interested in learning while in high school. I couldn't really appreciate a book until I was out of the classroom environment. It wasn't until I was in the Navy during the Korean War that I started to love literature. Learning took on a whole new meaning for me. Reading became something enjoyable and freeing. It was my time to escape into new worlds."

"Like counting for me."

"Yes, like counting. I had free time on the ship I was aboard and very little entertainment. My bunkmate, Bob Myers, was a college graduate and an English major, so he had plenty of books with him. And not just any old books, he had the great classics of the English language. Well, Bobby, he shared those books with me. But, not only did he share his books, he shared his knowledge. He made learning fun.

"On this ship I mentally explored new worlds. I was transported into different lands and cultures and time periods. Through those books I began to see the world in color. I discovered that setting is just one aspect of a novel. There are characters and plots and conflicts. There are metaphors and similes. You see, once I returned home, I had accumulated a vast array of knowledge, and enjoyed learning in the process. My bunkmate showed me that I had the potential to be educated. He showed me that I could learn, and even more so, that I wanted to learn."

"I do want to learn, too. I just wish I didn't have to worry so much about stuff like coal. I don't want to be gray like Radio Guy. Do you really think he's alive?"

"Yes, he is still alive. And so are you. I know the gray is hard to wade through. Sometimes when you are stuck in it, even the brightest lights can't help you navigate through it. You'll learn, though. That is a skill that those who have experienced the gray often perfect. When gray is presented in the future, you'll immediately look for color, while others remain stuck."

LEARNING FROM THE CHILD WITHIN

In the 1990s, San Antonio, Texas, was home to a true "hot war" between the Rupert Murdoch–owned *San Antonio Express-News* and the Hearst Corporation—owned *San Antonio Light*. Both newspapers were profitable and rocked along with always escalating competitive initiatives. Then came the Texas recession, during which literally all newspapers lost one-third of their ad revenues.

It was in this context that the *San Antonio Express-News* imported a consumer game from England called Wingo. Bingo-like cards were mailed to every home throughout Southwest Texas. Consumers matched the numbers on the cards with numbers published daily in the newspaper. The prizes offered helped boost the sales of the Sunday paper, which was the newspaper's real objective of the promotion. This boosted circulation numbers and created an advertiser perception of momentum and "winning" the newspaper battle.

The *San Antonio Light* offered a series of consumer promotions, but its weekly market research indicated that the Wingo game was the single most popular element in the market and was drawing a larger audience each week. The *San Antonio Light* was discouraged and sensed the prospect of losing the market battle because, in that recession environment, advertisers were increasingly choosing only one newspaper for their ads. That was the environment I entered when I visited San Antonio for a few days of creative brainstorming. At the end of the first day of my visit, the *San Antonio Light* editor, Ted Warmbold, asked if the group could stop at a museum where his curator friend had just launched a new exhibit of Mexican folk art. As the group walked through the exhibit, the curator and local community relations director explained the pieces of art.

When the group came to what looked like a gauze-covered board game, with carved elements adhered to it, the community relations director explained that the board depicted Loteria, which was a Mexican bingo that Mexican Americans grew up playing with their families.

At the time, San Antonio's population was 56 percent Mexican American. I turned to the *San Antonio Light's* publisher and said, "Loteria is our new game." Within weeks, the *San Antonio Light* launched the game. It became an instant success—vastly more popular than the competitor's Wingo. The tide turned and the *San Antonio Light's* circulation numbers and ad revenue soared. Not much later, Hearst acquired the Rupert Murdoch–owned *San Antonio Express-News*.

Between the Lines

Gray is a color and has a place in every landscape. The gray of life can be an invitation to pause, to re-assess, to reflect, to appreciate anew, and to not be so quick to judge.

I remember Bob Myers on that Navy ship sharing a book of poems from a favorite poet, Don Blanding, who was described as a vagabond poet living a simple life near the ocean in Hawaii. Bob and I shared one of his poems as a favorite:

> *"I used to think that I knew*
> *Day from night*
> *Black from white*
> *Wrong from right*
> *But as I grow from day to day*
> *I find that*
> *Gray comes in someway."*

chapter 10

A FATHER FIGURE

The lawn bowler's bowling ball spun out of control, escaping the straight path he had set for it. Perhaps it ricocheted off of an unexpected rock, or perhaps there was a patch of slick grass that caused it to slide off course. Despite the cause, his ball swerved toward our bench and was rolling to our feet.

"Oh look Bob, it's coming our way." Bobby's eyes lit up as if the ball had been laced in gold. He pushed up his glasses and sat up straight to prepare himself for its arrival.

"I see that." Though I saw the ball, I didn't quite see the reason for such excitement.

The man that trotted toward us was large in stature and in great physical condition. His broad shoulders and towering height undoubtedly commanded the attention of any room. His deep brown beard and strong jaw-line gave him a stately look, but his wavy hair softened him and made him approachable. I saw this man as a young professor plucked out of the 1940s, trotting on grass surrounded by ivy-covered brick buildings; his brown tweed blazer, khaki pants, and tasseled loafers made him an anachronism in the center of this modern-day city. He personified the smell of a cloistered room bulging with literature. A loud jet screamed overhead and I laughed at the timing.

Finally the bearded man caught up with the ball only a few feet from our bench. He smiled at us as he crouched down to pick it up, and nodded as he turned away to trot back.

"I wish that man was my dad." Bobby said.

"You do? Why is that?" I asked.

"He seems so colorful and fun. That would be a change from my life. I've never felt that cheery. I've never even known a man like that."

"Didn't you have any nice foster dads?" I asked.

"No, mostly women. Actually, I've never really had any dad in my life. The men that were part of the family never picked me up and hugged me. Or played baseball or football with me. They never showed me how they shaved their beards or tucked me in at night."

"I'm sorry to hear that."

"So instead I pretend that strangers are my dads. Sometimes I watch a dad with his son and picture him as my dad, too—how he would look when I scored my first home run after all that practicing, or how his face feels squished against mine after making honor roll in school. Other times I'll see a man that looks like he could be a father, but he has no kids with him. I imagine him as my dad, and that he is on his way to pick me up and take me out to dinner, or to buy me new shoes." Bobby paused, lost in thought. Perhaps he was dreaming of the man with the beard and the tasseled loafers. If I had to venture a guess, I would say Bobby was imagining the lawn bowler reading to him, maybe some Melville, perfecting character voices and background music. Or perhaps the child imagined the possible professor helping him study for a school test, or praising him for a stellar school report card.

"I know that none of them are really my dad," Bobby continued. "Its fun to pretend sometimes, but it makes me sad when I have to stop dreaming."

"You know Bobby, there have been many great men in my life who have taught me important life lessons, showing me how to be a loyal employee, compassionate friend, and gracious gentleman. Just by closing my eyes, I can see so many of their faces now. There was Charlie Bechard, the circulation manager at the *Times Union,* who guided me as a teenage office boy. And Perren Hayes, the classified ad manager, who encouraged me to accept my first advertising sales job. Oh the list could go on. So many men who have supported my actions and inspired my creativity and confidence. Good men, colorful men, who made my life less and less grey. Though he was not a tall man, Gene Robb, the former publisher of the *Times Union* was a towering figure who, in particular, left a subtle, but permanent imprint on my life, like a watermark on fine paper. He didn't just touch my life, he guided me as well."

Learning from the Child Within

Gene Robb pulled me out from the pack when I was a young advertising salesman at the *Times Union*. I was studying English literature at Siena

College at night and had begun publishing small pieces in the college's literary journal, under the name R. Danzig.

Mr. Robb was on the board of trustees at Siena College, and, therefore, received every publication the college printed, including the literary journal. One day, we were riding on the elevator at the paper when he turned to me and said, "I see an R. Danzig at Siena College writing for its journal, the *Beverwyck*."

I told him I went to Siena College at night. Our conversation ended there, but Gene Robb subsequently did something one might not be able to do today. He became intrigued because I was a successful young salesman who was going to college at night as an English major—a subject dear to his heart. Without my knowledge, he had my grades sent to him after every semester."

When I graduated from Siena College in 1962, Mr. Robb asked me to join him for breakfast one Saturday morning. He told me that it was his intention to retire from the publisher's position in 1974. It was over breakfast that I learned that he had been keeping an eye on me.

And like a father passing down his company to his son, he told me the he had concluded that he wanted me to be an optional candidate to succeed him. "With that in mind," he said, "I am going to put you in a program where you'll go into the various disciplines of the newspaper. But, the deal will be, that whatever job you go into, if you can't cut it, you can't go

back to the old job. You're not going to be a crown prince. You really have to perform every assignment."

Mr. Robb nominated me for a Stanford University Fellowship in Journalism and I became one of twelve recipients. When I returned from Stanford University, I became general manager of a small paper, which the *Times Union* had recently acquired in Schenectady, New York. That was in 1969. Mr. Robb died suddenly that August.

To my surprise, according to his wishes, I succeeded him as publisher. At first, it was bewildering for me to walk into the office that was once his. He taught me the importance of investing in people and not just in work. And, as he became a role model, he offered me something I didn't have in my personal life, guidance similar to what a father might offer a son.

BETWEEN THE LINES

Learn to recognize and value nurturers in your life and celebrate their friendship. Avoid pretending that such relationships exist. Give life to the family and friendship bonds for which you yearn. When you are open, those people will find you.

chapter 11

CAMOUFLAGE

The man clipping the lawn was taking his job seriously. Perhaps he wanted the ground to reflect the sky's blanketing warmth. Or perhaps the blue, crisp breeze deserved to take with it a green, crisp smell. Despite the reasons he had for caring, the man was diligent. He inspected the ground where the grass met the flowerbed, brushing his hand over each bordering blade. He moved cautiously on his hands and knees, keenly aware of the suffering grass he crushed beneath his mat. He attempted not to drag his legs as he crawled forward to comb and clip the awaiting lawn. Instead, he waddled right and left as he exaggeratingly picked his hands and knees off the ground.

Bobby disrupted my gazing. "That man sure is working hard," he said.

"Yes, yes he is." I replied. I had almost forgotten that Bobby was next to me on the bench. I wondered if the boy could appreciate the care the man was putting into his work. "He seems to enjoy what he is doing."

"I guess so. He looks kind of funny."

"He must have his reasons. Would you like to take a walk?" I wanted to give the man space as he trimmed out his masterpiece.

"Sure."

As we walked along Bobby seemed hesitant to speak. But, as if a gust of wind pushed out his breath, the boy began. "Bob, have you ever been ashamed before?"

"Ashamed? Of other people?" I thought the child was still thinking of the man clipping the grass; my mind was with his diligence and his care, with his waddling crawl. I assumed Bobby's was also.

"Well . . ." Bobby seemed hesitant. He looked at his feet and started to move his mouth without making a sound. Ironically, he seemed ashamed to go on.

"I try not to judge others Bobby. I try as best as I can to—"

"No Bob, I mean you. Ashamed of yourself." His eyes barely clipped mine as he turned to look away. I didn't know what to say. I thought I heard a sniffle, but I couldn't tell if his cheeks were wet. A mind-scrambling silence followed and blocked any consoling or probing words that could come out of my mouth. I contemplated whistling to mask the fact that I couldn't answer, couldn't comfort, couldn't help the boy. But whistling wouldn't have been appropriate. I wasn't quite sure what he was really asking, but I knew I had gone wrong with my answer.

We passed some kiosks that were preparing to open. Bobby walked over to one. He was escaping the silence, he must have been, for there was nothing to look at but the zipped up covering. But the boy looked anyway, and not just looked . . . his eyes rummaged through the hidden contents. Then he moved onto the next boarded up stand only to shop through the opaque canvas.

"Bobby, I didn't mean to misunderstand you. I'm sure I have been ashamed before, son, but I really can't think of a particular time. I'm sorry, I wish I could be of—"

"Well I can think of one." The boy continued to look at the kiosk. He talked to the canvas.

"I'd like to hear it if you want to tell me about it. If not then—"

"It was a few years back. I lived with a lady who lived alone in a house . . ." The boy cut off again as he moved to the next kiosk. "An ugly house. Old. Creaky, wooden house." Bobby's eyes looked watery. "Poor. Dirty, three-story house. Six of them. In a row. All of them poor looking. All of them ugly. All of them the same. And it wouldn't have been so bad if they weren't the only ones."

The child moved to the neighboring kiosk. Once he planted himself in front of the next, he began again, "But that's it, you see. All the other homes were different. Nice. They had fences. Had lawns. Had flowers. Had families."

He uprooted himself from the closed kiosks and walked along the path. I hurried to walk near him. "She lived on the third floor. The whole house wasn't even hers. And I was embarrassed of it. Of the house. Of where I lived. I was ashamed. And not just a little ashamed. I got on the school bus blocks away so that I didn't have to stand in front of my poor house. Instead, I waited in front of the picket fences. I waited in front of the lawns and the flowers so that everyone thought I came out of those homes . . . thought that my family was watching me inside the windows with the pretty curtains. And I came home off the bus at the same spot, where my make believe family waited for me with an after school snack." Bobby stopped.

The boy was discombobulated. It was as if a tornado blew through his peaceful picket-fenced picture. He shrugged his shoulders and pushed his glasses onto the bridge of his nose. "Why was I so ashamed, Bob?"

I didn't know if the boy wanted an answer. Maybe he was ashamed because his difference from the other boys became physically tangible, physically viewable for all to see. But how could I say that in a way the kid could understand?

"Why do I still feel so guilty, Bob?"

Should I speak? Should I offer an answer? Maybe he was so guilty because he knew he shouldn't be ashamed of anyone, especially of a woman opening her doors to an orphan boy, and especially of the orphan boy himself. I opened my mouth to speak, but the child kept going.

"I hid where I lived from everyone. But, it was so tiring to pretend. I didn't want to walk to the nice homes. I really didn't. I wanted to just get on the bus at the corner of the creaky, wooden ones. The poor ones. But I was afraid of what all the other kids would say." Bobby wiped his face, pushed up his glasses and continued, "Then one day when I was at home the foster lady told me I had a surprise on the way. I asked her what it was, but she refused to say. I was so excited. I couldn't imagine what it could be. When the doorbell rang, she went downstairs to answer it. I could hear from the bottom of the stairs the footsteps of a few people. Then that's when I heard him. I thought maybe I should run somewhere and hide. But it was too late. They were almost to the living room. Tommy, a boy in my class, came through the door with his mother. I was so ashamed to have my classmate in my house. He knew. Everyone would know . . ."

As we retraced our earlier steps to return to our bench, we again passed the kiosks. This time all of their items were exposed and people were browsing the stands. There were porcelain dolls for sale in one cart, paperback books in another. Chinese figurines filled a booth while

handbags, jewelry, perfumes and herbal teas were in stalls of their own. The items in the kiosks brought life and color to the park path.

"Tommy and I went out to play that day for hours. We played all sorts of games. We went all over the neighborhood. It was so much fun. And when his mom came to pick him up, all they said was, 'See you soon!' That was it. Tommy still wanted to be friends with me after seeing where I lived. That just made me feel more ashamed about walking to the houses with the picket fences and not standing in front of my own dried-up lawn. But I stopped hiding and took the bus at a new stop, the one on my corner."

"You know, Bobby," people camouflage their feelings and different issues throughout their lives. But in the end, they blind themselves and others to the real good. You have to learn to be yourself, rather than what you think other people want you to be.

When Bobby and I reached the bench again, the man who pruned and trimmed and clipped the grounds was gone. The fruits of his labor were visible signs of his hidden presence. But, I wondered, would any passerby know just how diligent the man was? Would anyone realize just how much effort he put into this plot of land? Perhaps not. Perhaps no one will ever appreciate how difficult it was to achieve that pristine landscape. Perhaps no one will even notice the landscape at all. But I was sure that whenever that man walked past this park, he would see more than just grass.

Learning from the Child Within

Soon after I became the publisher of the *Times Union* and *Knickerbocker News*, I received a phone call from then New York governor, Nelson Rockefeller. Governor Rockefeller explained that the legislature had been deadlocked for a few months in passing the annual state budget required by law. He explained the pivotal, deciding vote belonged to the state senator from the Albany area and then asked me to call the senator and ask that he cast a "yes" vote.

The governor believed the senator would follow my lead if I told him a yes vote was the right vote to cast. Governor Rockefeller added that he and the entire state of New York would be indebted to me if I would help.

As a relatively new publisher, I felt somewhat intimidated by the governor's personal request. After all, only the governor, the state senator and I would know of my phone call, suggesting a vote had no appearance of being the wrong thing to do.

On the other hand, as the local newspaper publisher, if I made a request to a local politician, it might cause him to conclude that he had done me a favor and he could expect favorable coverage in the newspaper.

I thought that proposition through and decided not to involve myself in the legislative decision-making process. I called the governor and explained my decision to him. Although I could have privately camouflaged

a phone call to the state senator, it was not the right thing to do to maintain the unfettered independence of the newspaper.

This was not my only camouflage incident with Governor Rockefeller. Each time, however, when shown that he was heading toward camouflage, he reassessed his position.

Governor Rockefeller saw the possibility of a state capital presence, the Empire Plaza, which would inspire pride in state employees and visitors to Albany. Although the beneficial impact to the project on the city of Albany was immense, the Governor's version of a new downtown, complete with government offices, did have some flaws.

Originally called the South Mall, the enormous project, with its magnificent architecture and sweeping scope, covered a vast downtown area. Gleaming marble would replace the faded Albany core, the way cartoonist often replace pictures of an old year, with a new year—in a single stroke at midnight.

Planning was precise and professional. Everything about the South Mall project would inspire awe and admiration. Once a person encountered that inspiring architecture, mind, body and soul would be elevated. The design appeared flawless.

However, in the assessment of the two papers for which I was the publisher, a gaping flaw persisted in the backdrop to the South Mall. What good is a flawless diamond if it is set in the rough? How can you have marble facades when the houses of the neighboring buildings are crumbling?

Articles and editorials urged the state government to include the surrounding decaying neighborhoods as a part of Albany's renaissance.

Governor Rockefeller again called me. He asked me to join him for lunch to discuss the newspapers' accounts and comments. Aside from a few pleasantries, he went straight to his point and said he was terribly disappointed with the negative spin our newspapers were putting on this most important initiative designed to benefit the very city that housed our newspapers.

He said it was outrageous for us to place the spotlight on the surrounding neighborhoods since the heart of the project was the new state office building complex. He said he was certain I would see his point if we could only talk it through. I said he might well be right, but that I would like to continue our discussion in his chauffeured car while I gave his driver directions.

He agreed and off we went. With my directions, Governor Rockefeller's chauffeur drove the limousine through neglected, half-abandoned neighborhoods with the State building hovering over them like a guilty conscience. I pointed to the rundown homes and said that each morning the people living in those dreadful circumstances would step out of their homes, look up in any direction, and see a sight like Oz. Yet, when they looked at their immediate surroundings, they would conclude that their lives would go untouched by the great changes emerging before their eyes. After a few minutes of silence, Governor Rockefeller told me he had never traveled that way before.

When we returned to the driveway of the Governor's mansion, I turned to him and said that our newspapers were thrilled he had chosen Albany as the site of what would be the most striking state complex in the nation. I said it would be an absolute gem, but to ignore the surrounding neighborhoods in the restoration process would be to place that jewel in a cesspool. He repeated that exact phrase to me—a jewel in a cesspool.

The next day, he announced a new neighborhood commission for the South Mall project. He inspired the commission to enlarge the boundaries of the initiative so it included upgrades of the surrounding neighborhoods; he inspired the design of the jewel's setting to maximize its shine.

Although some might have thought Governor Rockefeller was camouflaging an issue he didn't want to face, he really just needed someone to pull back the camouflage others had inadvertently created for him by never offering him a personal look at the surrounding neighborhoods.

BETWEEN THE LINES

When those small gray areas emerge in our lives and we are tempted to camouflage the truth, we only cover up the issue and invite further difficulty. When we learn to accept reality and face the truth, we invite symmetry, clarity and purpose.

Camouflage doesn't make a problem go away; it just saves it for another day.

chapter 12

SECOND BREATH

It was a raw day. I walked briskly. The wind burned my face. On the park path I could hear nothing but my lungs filling with air. Everything I passed seemed to be a silent activity. A little girl whispered a secret story to her sister while a middle-aged man walked his dog. A young lady ran by with music reserved for her own ears, and several college students leisurely tossed a Frisbee, separated by yards of open grass. As the scenery changed, the sound of my breath remained the only noise that echoed in my ears. Staccato puffs of clouds left my mouth. To an onlooker, I was engaged in my own silent activity.

"Wait up," a small voice cried out. My breath went off beat and the patterns became irregular. I looked over my shoulder to see Bobby jogging toward me. He appeared winded. I wondered how long he had been trying to catch up.

"Hi Bob," he spoke thickly and swallowed hard. I slowed down my pace.

"How are you doing today, son?"

"Tired from chasing you."

"I'm sorry. I didn't see you there behind me."

"It's ok. Why are you walking so fast?" Bobby asked.

"I don't know really. Guess I just felt like it. Kind of refreshing to clean your lungs of all the stale air—like a second breath."

"A second breath?"

"Hmm. A revitalization of life. An invigorating renewal. If that makes any sense."

Bobby shuffled along trying to keep up with me. Though my pace was slower, he was still skipping here and there between strides, trying to stay in step with me. "I have second breaths all the time. I move a lot. I've moved more times than I can count. And every time I go to a new home it's filled with strangers. The mom's new, the dad's new, and all the brothers and sisters are new. They are new faces and new ways of doing things. Some like the floors really clean; some like their shoes shined. Some don't care either way about those things. Some are quiet; others are loud. Some are nice; some are mean to me. I know they all try, but some try harder than others. And it isn't just the families that are strangers. I have a strange bed and strange food. The town's strange. The school's strange. The teacher's strange and all the other kids are strange." Bobby stopped speaking for a moment to catch his breath.

"It sounds like you have to adjust and adapt to life often. I'm sure that you have been successful at it though. Every new endeavor is overwhelming in the beginning for everyone."

"I just wish it didn't have to happen so often. Changing families is hard work. And when I go to a new home I get nervous and scared. No matter how many times I do it, in the beginning I think that I'll never feel at home; I think that everyone and everything will always be strangers. But then I take a second breath. I tell myself that I can do it, that I will figure it out. I come up with ways to remember their names and what they like and don't like. I try to learn the town and schoolyard and the best way to get there. I think up plans and ways to feel comfortable. But first I need to start fresh and unscared. I just sometimes get too scared to remember where to start again."

Remaining beside me, Bobby was doing his best to keep up with me. I knew exactly what he meant by a second breath. Invigorating renewal. Perhaps at his age it was not so invigorating, but it was indeed a form of restoration, a way to make his broken life feel whole, his weakened self feel strong.

"I'm tired, Bob," the boy said in shallow gasps.

"Sorry, I'll slow down." I, too, was wheezing. "Bobby, what happened to your first breath?"

"It's never deep enough."

I stopped walking and looked at Bobby. "Sometimes you have to push through the first breath in order to reach an opportunity to take a deeper, much-needed second breath." Bobby smiled and we took a long, deep second breath together.

Learning from the Child Within

The Hearst-owned *Boston Herald* had long-negotiated labor union contracts in association with the much larger *Boston Globe*. When I became CEO of the Hearst Newspaper Group, it was my personal view that over a long period of time, the *Globe's* acceptance of highly restrictive and very costly labor contracts had a punitive cost impact on the smaller revenue base of the *Herald*. In fact, I believed that prior corporate newspaper management had seen no alternative but to accept those labor cost burdens and just swim upstream, hoping to someday become a profitable business.

I concluded we would no longer have labor bargaining together with the *Globe*. We could not continue to accept labor cost burdens or pretend we could run on the same track with the much larger *Globe* newspaper.

I told our local Boston newspaper management of our new corporate view. They immediately worried that the unions would demand more concessions of us. They thought that by bargaining alone, the *Herald* could not afford to have a strike occur.

Our local management was authorized to be very transparent and open with the union leaders. There was to be broad understanding of the financial peril that was the reality of the *Herald* situation.

I went to Boston and had breakfast at the Ritz Carlton Hotel with the CEO of the *Globe*. I told him that the *Herald* would no longer bargain with the *Globe*, and would go its own way with union bargaining. The CEO looked directly into my eyes and said, "You cannot do that. We must find a way to muddle through this current round of negotiations and then talk about splitting the labor efforts sometime in the future."

I took a second breath and told him, "No. The *Globe*, has been the muddler and the *Herald* has been the mudlee. That day is over."

The *Herald* began to bargain with the unions and was open about its heavy losses. I found that the union leadership—long accustomed to the local *Herald* management "poor mouthing" for decades—did not believe that the *Herald* would face them down and risk a strike. Our analysis told us that if a strike occurred causing a failure of the newspaper, our severance pay costs to union members would exceed twelve million dollars. Our physical plant and real estate was estimated to be worth six million. Therefore, a strike-induced plant closure could cause a net loss of six-million dollars.

After months of fruitless negotiations, it was obvious that the unions did not believe the *Herald's* leadership—they had spent too many years accepting punishing economic contracts for decades when bargaining with the *Globe*. Simultaneously, I concluded that only an outside new owner of the newspaper might have the credibility to convince the unions to change. Work practice changes needed to eliminate labor waste and reduce operating costs by an estimated 12 million dollars a year were needed to save the newspaper's voice for the Boston community and to save all the at-risk jobs.

Our team detailed the wasted costs union by union and produced a book with specific labor changes required in the contracts. We engaged a business broker to search for a new buyer. In the final analysis only News Corporation and its chief executive officer Rupert Murdoch were willing to take on the uphill challenge of dealing with the unions and attempt to save the newspaper. News Corporation, of course, had no history with the unions. News Corporation had no reason to continue the effort unless they had labor cost relief and no severance cost penalty should the union resist and the newspaper close down. The twelve million-dollar severance cost would belong to our Hearst newspaper.

We told the unions that we had decided to leave the Boston newspaper market and that News Corporation had emerged as the only possible new owner and publisher. News Corporation's agreement to continue the newspaper was directly linked to the unions agreeing to eliminate wasteful contracts.

Using the detailed book of cost changes needed, union by union, News Corporation began to bargain with the clock ticking. All agreements had to be completed within two weeks. One by one, the unions came to agreement.

Only one union remained with open issues. The printer's union, whose president had resisted all changes in labor conditions. With only that single union remaining, Rupert Murdoch went to Boston and joined his bargaining team for one last bargaining session attempt to save the paper.

I was manning our labor desk at the publisher's office, staying in contact every 30 minutes with our corporate chief executive officer in New York City until very late at night. It was about three o'clock in the morning when Rupert Murdoch called to tell me that the printer's union president would not budge—even though all the other eleven unions had agreed to the changes. He was calling to let me know that he was going back to the negotiation room to tell all the unions the bargaining was over and he was leaving Boston. News Corporation would be out of the picture.

I waited and took a second breath.

I asked Rupert Murdoch to give me an hour and then let me join him at the negotiation hotel room to make that announcement together. He agreed. I then instructed our Boston newspaper management to shut down the presses and evacuate the building. The press had never been shut down in the entire history of the newspaper. It stunned everyone. It sent a message to all the union negotiators at the hotel.

I then went to the hotel and asked Rupert and the full management bargaining team to join me in the large room packed with the union committees from all eleven unions. I introduced myself. I told them that the *Herald* had shut down the presses for the first time ever. I thanked the unions for their efforts to reach new agreements and save both their jobs and the newspaper itself. I then walked directly to face the printer's union president and said, "I thank every one here except you. You alone have cost all these jobs. You alone have cost all these employees their income. You alone have killed the *Boston Herald*."

He jumped up, raised his hand and almost screamed, "I agree. I agree to the changes." Then he gulped and took a second breath.

All the new contracts were signed that night. The jobs were saved and with that cost relief the *Herald* was able to become a viable business and continue to publish in Boston every day.

Cee

Between the Lines

When emotion and uncertainty visit your doorstep, step back, take a second breath, and allow your emotions to settle before taking action.

Cee

chapter 13

MOMENTS OF SHINING "AND FAMILY"

It was an unusual day. Though it was an early summer's morning, the sun's heat foreshadowed the strong warmth to come. As I walked along the path, I was thankful for nature's umbrellas; the trees offered pockets of cool shade that sporadically dotted the trail. A faint breeze ruffled the leaves, causing some light to penetrate the shadows.

This was not merely a routine visit to the park, but an impromptu weekend spent in the city with my wife. Inspired by the spontaneity of the vacation, I decided to go off the beaten bench.

Bobby was waiting for me at the lawn bowlers' field. I wasn't quite sure how he knew I would be around this Sunday morning, but I was glad to see him. His young spirit was more refreshing than the shade of all of nature's umbrellas.

"Hi Bob!" He seemed to almost skip with boyish exuberance when he saw me on the path.

"Hello there, son," I could hear a smile in my own voice. "How are you today?"

"Very good. I'm doing very very good today. Can I walk with you?"

"Very very good?" I smiled at Bobby and he nodded at me. "Yes. Walk with me. That would be great."

"I'm glad I saw you, Bob. I wanted to run into you today."

"You know, I had the same thoughts."

As we walked away from the lawn bowlers, away from the familiar bench, we continued in silence. It wasn't an awkward stillness, pregnant with tension, but a mutual appreciation for the peace gained, for the friendship formed, and for the memories shared. Words were no longer needed to convey the comfort we felt. Bobby kicked a rock and followed behind in the wake of its rising dirt. I picked up a helicopter-like leaf and spun it through the air. We continued in this manner for about ten minutes, rocks punted, leaves swirled, with the faint breeze offering direction to our sports. Finally I shattered the silence.

"Hey, Bobby?"

"Yeah?"

"I was wondering if you remembered something—or someone, to be exact."

"I might, what is it Bob? Or who is it?"

"Well, you see, I remember this social worker. She was a middle-aged lady, blonde with some gray patches running through her hair, tall, with sharp, bony features—one of the social workers during my younger years. And, you see, Bobby, this woman once said to me words that made a lasting impression. She said, and now, you can correct me if I'm wrong here, but she said to me, 'You are worthwhile.' Just like that, she uttered such a simple, pure sentence. But the funny thing is, the reason I remember it so vividly is because I know she meant it. I could tell she was genuine and sincere. She truly wanted me to know that I, Bobby Danzig, was worthwhile. She had no motive for saying what she did. I had nothing to offer, she had nothing to gain. I was worthwhile—not because I would shine shoes. I was worthwhile—not because I would carry coal. I was worthwhile—not because I would make no trouble. Just me, I mattered."

Bobby replied with a hint of a smirk.

"So you do know who I'm referring to."

"Yeah, but I don't know about her being sharp. She seems really soft to me."

I chuckled. "You're right, son, maybe she wasn't so sharp as I remember. But I will never forget the words. And, even more than the words, the sincerity in which they were spoken." I picked up another leaf and spun it in the wind. "And you want to hear something else?"

"Sure."

"Several years ago, when I had become publisher of the newspaper, I went back to visit Mae." Curiosity and disbelief caused Bobby's eyes to widen. "I found her in a nursing home. You see, I wanted to thank her for her words. I needed to show her that she was right, that I was worthwhile. So, I found her, frail and old. They had set her up in the parlor chair of the nursing home. She beamed when I walked in. I can see her so clearly, her knit shawl hung over her shoulders. I walked over to her and put my hands in hers. Before I could utter a word, she said to me, 'Didn't I always tell you that you are worthwhile?' I was in awe. I told her how I looked forward to this day—the day when I could share with her my gratitude for the confidence and value she placed in me. I said to her, 'In a life stuck in the shadows, you, Mae Morse, gave me my first shining moment that penetrated the darkness.' We discussed our lives and the value we found in them each day."

"I'm glad you got to see her. I always was taught that it's important to say thank you."

"Never forget that Bobby." I said, my mind still in the nursing home sitting with Mae and her knit shawl.

In the meantime, Bobby picked up a new sport. He bounced in and out of the patches of sunlight, skipping over the shadow and landing two-footed in the brightness. He paused in a purely circular spot of light and turned to the trees. He stretched out his arms and began to boom, "Ladies and gentlemen, welcome to a night where talent abounds and fun never ceases, where boys and girls reveal their gifts for the arts, and the not so artful still entertain. Where people come to see ordinary citizens become extraordinary performers. Where the musician, the comedian, and the actor come to dazzle. Welcome to all who have stepped in this arena, for, amused you will be and delighted you will leave!"

The boy held my attention. I was compelled to clap. He spoke so clearly, so forcefully. I didn't think he had it in him. He commanded that spot on the path. He illuminated what was already lit. I continued to clap as I asked, "Bobby, where did you learn that?"

"In school," he mumbled as he sheepishly left the sunlight patch and hung his head. A bit of embarrassment set in.

"In school? That's it? And what was it for?" We continued walking.

"It was a circus we performed in school. Our English teacher, Miss Burke, ran a spring talent show every year, and for my year the theme was the circus. I was the ringmaster. Those were my opening lines."

"That was very impressive. You must have given a wonderful performance."

"I was so scared. I couldn't believe it when Miss Burke asked me to be the ringmaster. She told me that I was good with words. She said that I would be able to bring all the acts together. I was the narrator, I guess you can say. I had so much fun doing it, though. I dressed the part and everything."

"What did you wear?"

"Well, I had a job setting up bowling pins, so I took that money and bought myself a ringmaster's outfit. I wore riding pants, a yellow jacket, a pair of riding boots, and a white collared shirt. Miss Burke gave me a top hat to add the final touch. It was really something."

"It sounds like you worked hard."

"I did. Every day. I practiced on my own, and I met with Miss Burke all winter until I felt ready to perform. And I worried a lot, too. I was so afraid that the foster family would want to get rid of me before the performance. I wanted to be the ringmaster so bad. But I also didn't want to disappoint Miss Burke. I knew that she was counting on me. I knew the class was counting on me, too." Bobby paused, the look of anguish upon his face proved he was reliving the fear. Once his eyebrows unfurled, he continued, "In the end, it all worked out. I wasn't moved before the show."

"It sounds like a great opportunity. Miss Burke must have really believed in you to give you that kind of responsibility."

"She did. After the performance in front of the entire school, Miss Burke asked me to step forward and stand next to her. Then she asked the whole school to give me special recognition for 'using words so beautifully to frame this special event and guide us all through a grand day at the circus.' The entire student body stood up and applauded me. I never thought I liked the spotlight before, but it felt good to be shining out of the crowd for once."

"Yeah, we all love those moments of light, Bobby. Everyone deserves to shine."

The boy found another rock waiting to meet the tip of his shoe. I found myself a leaf to twirl in the faint breeze. We walked together underneath nature's umbrellas.

LEARNING FROM THE CHILD WITHIN

When I joined the *Times Union*, the colleagues of that newspaper became my family. Happily we were also part of the Hearst Corporation which, when I joined the corporate group, had a strong, constant overarching sense of family. It gave one a feeling of being part of a nurtured place—always caring for colleagues while concurrently holding performance standards to a high level.

For example, when I became publisher of the *Times Union*, my predecessor had endured some health challenges and was unable to monitor inter-departmental conflicts as closely as he would have were his health more robust. The newspaper was "plagued with executive competition." At weekly management sessions, I noticed how the executives guarded their thank you

own departmental turf and bristled when other managers made suggestions for departments outside their own.

The net effect was a type of paralysis that allowed the company to function each day, but inhibited any collective quest for new growth. Not one of the executives was a force for progress in the collective purpose of the newspaper since all their concentration was on their own feet—in their own shoes exclusively. The organization had no feeling of family. It did not shine.

After a few weeks of struggling with the tensions, I approached the American Press Institute, a newspaper executive development resource. I asked that executives be permitted to attend sessions in areas of responsibility different from their own. For example, an editor would attend a session for advertising managers. When I told the competing managers that they would be attending these sessions and learn to "walk in the other person's shoes," reaction was universally negative.

Within a few months of genuinely learning about the challenges of each other's specialty areas, they began a new language of insight, understanding, and cooperation. Within six months, we had committees working collectively on new horizons. We had achieved family cohesion— and worked seamlessly as that circus of my childhood had years earlier— though we all played different roles and executed a wide variety of initiatives at the same time, we were all moving in the same direction.

When Frank Bennack Jr. was named the CEO of the Hearst Newspaper Group, he began what would become quarterly group meetings of all the Hearst newspaper publishers. Agendas were advanced, lessons were shared, and a collegiality began to be fueled. Each newspaper would host a meeting in that paper's local city. Two social events, which also invited the spouses of the publishers, followed the business meetings. One took place at the local publisher's home and the other at some local institution that highlighted an attraction of that city. Family spirit grew.

When Frank Bennack was then named president and corporate CEO of the entire Hearst Corporation, and I succeeded him as CEO of the Hearst Newspaper Group, one of my early priorities was to sustain and enlarge that sense of family among all our Hearst newspapers. In my twenty-year privilege of heading the company that family focus remained a high priority.

As we acquired new newspaper properties, an early priority was to visit the new member of the family often, arrange to meet our new employees and colleagues, make ourselves available for their questions and walk the plant to meet staffers. We also made it a practice to hold a community leader dinner dance with premier entertainment. We would make brief welcoming remarks, introduce our board members and senior Hearst management, tell them we appreciated that as new owners we were guests in the family of their community, and we would work to be good citizens and bring pride to that family.

Despite the size of the paper and its local city—from Houston, Texas, to Bad Axe, Michigan—we always made the same effort to salute the local family and earn our acceptance as new owners of their newspaper.

As we grew to six thousand employee/colleagues, I took my early yearning for family and shining moments and infused them into my own efforts to sustain both ideals. For example, I regularly sent complimentary notes to our staffers all over the nation when advised of some special contribution or achievement. In fact, I would take a list of their names and achievements home on the train at night and write handwritten notes to each, putting a "T" or "F" next to certain names where special contributions had been made.

I sent the handwritten notes to their home addresses because I believe a note from the head of the newspaper company, opened at home where they were loved, would give each person a fresh spotlight of recognition in front of their own family. When I brought the list back to my longtime administrative assistant, Marge Murphy, she knew the "F" meant flowers to be sent to that colleague's spouse with the same note to each. "Congratulations on the good news for your (Mary or John, etc.) Bob Danzig." The "T" was for extraordinary achievement and would tell Marge to send a Tiffany gift appropriate for a female or male spouse with the very same note of congratulations.

Did it matter? Well, I can tell you this, that as I was preparing to step down after my twenty year run and hand the wheels to my long time deputy, George Irish, he told me he had saved every note I had ever sent to him over those years.

My sense of family was nurtured and valuable. I am not sure I would have had the same intensity of reaching to create that family sense had I not had such a longing for that family value in all those years when I had none—and had I not had the early ringmaster taste of a shining moment.

BETWEEN THE LINES

Organizations are collections of individual talent, aspirations, home circumstances, and backgrounds. When the leader reaches with constancy and personalized focus to create an ongoing sense of family, it causes the individual to choose to give more.

chapter 14

PURPOSEFUL PERSISTENCE

The snow was coming down heavy now. It had already blanketed the city in about eight inches and the number was continuing to rise. Central park was filled with quite a few bundled-up children and their parents. Yet, despite the stiff stick-like kids with only their eyes exposed, there seemed to be a peaceful calm that fell upon the park.

Bobby was beside me in his thin winter coat. The boy looked surprisingly rosy despite his lack of layers.

"Did you ever make snow angels before, Bobby?"

"Snow angels? You mean like snowmen?"

"No, not really. You don't build them like you build snowmen, you sort of sculpt them out of your own body."

"Hmm." Bobby thought for a moment before he responded. "No, I don't think I've ever made a snow angel before."

"Want to learn how?"

"Sure."

"Ok, first you have to lie down in the snow, like so." I sat down in the snow and slipped on to my back. I had forgotten how chilly it could be to make such a divine creature. I tugged on my scarf to protect my exposed neck. "Now don't sit so close to me. We need room on either side of us to make the angels."

"Is here ok?" Bobby asked.

"A little further, about five feet away. Right there, that is fine. Are you all settled, Bobby?"

"I'm ready. What's next?"

"Now we are going to make the angel. You have to raise your arms over your head, and move your legs out from side to side as if you were doing jumping jacks. And then bring your arms back to your sides and your feet and legs together again. Keep repeating the jumping jacks over and over again until I say stop." I looked over at Bobby to see if he was copying me properly. Like a good student, he was perfecting the art of angel making. He had his mouth open, attempting to catch some of the falling snow on his tongue.

"How ahm ah ooing 'Ob? oay?" Bobby asked with his tongue still protruding.

"You're doing great, son." I couldn't believe that no one before this day had ever made an angel with Bobby. It was a bittersweet moment to think that I was the first. And who am I really to this boy? Am I just a dream? Will he forget me—forget that I had made it through life even though I lived his suffering? Will he be comforted by my ambition, my success, and my reassurances? Or is he solely here for me? So that I might be appreciative of where I am now and from where I came? Is his life my lesson only? Or is my life his lesson also? "Okay, you can stop now, kid."

Mid-raise of the arms, Bobby stopped in his tracks and bounced up in anticipation.

"Alright, now Bobby, take a giant step out of the angel so that you don't ruin him."

"It's a boy angel, Bob?"

"Or ruin her, whichever."

"No it matters."

"It does?"

"Yes, so that I can name it."

"Well, of course then Bobby, yeah, sure, so that you can name it." Seemed like a logical thought, though I had never named a snow angel before.

"Do you know what I would name mine?" the boy asked. We were in an awkward stance. We both stood with our feet apart in the bottom of the angel skirt. Neither of us took that giant step out.

"I'm going to guess a woman's name, though I'm not sure of the specifics."

"I'll tell you. My angel's name is Mrs. Foreman."

"Mrs. Foreman, huh? Did you just make that up?"

"No she was one of my foster moms."

"And you liked her?"

"Yeah. She was one of the nice ones. She said the nicest thing to me once. I remember on my first day in her home she just said the nicest thing. She sat me down at her kitchen table in front of cookies and milk and said that she knew it was hard for me to keep moving—to go from family to family to family. She said that she knew it took persistence. But she said that I was going to bring a lot to her family. She said that I was going to be a new face that brought new happiness, new thoughts, new growth. Yeah, that's what she said. That I was unique and that I was a gift to her and her family. She said that she wanted me to know that the gift of being me should bring purpose to my persistence. She made me feel worthy."

"Well then Bobby, in light of your story, I think Mrs. Foreman is a great name. Now, just take a giant step out and you can look at your angel."

But instead of stepping out in front of his angel, Bobby jumped a few feet to the side of Mrs. Foreman and began to lie down.

"Son, what are you doing?

"I'm making another."

"Don't you want to look at your angel?"

"No, I don't need to see it, I can picture her face right now. I'd rather get started on another. I like this. Make an angel for all your angels."

I had never thought of it that way. "Who is this one, kid?"

"You."